MOTHERS AND THEIR ADOPTED CHILDREN—
THE BONDING PROCESS

Mothers and Their Adopted Children — the Bonding Process

SECOND EDITION

Dorothy W. Smith, R.N., Ed.D., F.A.A.N.
Professor of Nursing, College of Nursing, Rutgers University

Laurie N. Sherwen, R.N., Ph.D.
Director, The Maternal-Infant Core Competency Project, March of Dimes Birth Defects Foundation

The Tiresias Press, Inc.
New York City

Copyright © 1988
The Tiresias Press, Inc.
116 Pinehurst Ave., New York City 10033

Printed in U.S.A.

Library of Congress Catalog Card Number: 87-051227
International Standard Book Number: 0-913292-40-0

ABOUT THE AUTHORS

Dorothy W. Smith, R.N., Ed.D., F.A.A.N., has published extensively in nursing and has presented papers and conducted workshops both here and abroad. Among her books are: *Pharmacology and Drug Therapy in Nursing* (co-authored with Morton Rodman), *Care of the Adult Patient, Perspectives on Clinical Teaching,* and *Survival of Illness.* Her adoption of two daughters, as a single parent, led to an interest in the bonding process and to the study on which this book is based.

Laurie N. Sherwen, R.N., Ph.D., is Director of a federally funded grant, The Maternal-Infant Core Competency Project, which has developed content and skills in maternal-infant nursing for baccalaureate curriculum. Formerly Coordinator of The Parent-Child Graduate Nursing Program at Rutgers College, her extensive writings on pregnancy and parenting include two recent books, *Analysis and Application of Nursing Research: Parent-Neonate Studies* and *Psychosocial Dimensions of the Pregnant Family*.

Contents

DEDICATION

Dorothy W. Smith: to her daughters, Shannon and Helena

Laurie Nehls Sherwen: to her parents, Marjory Nehls and William F. Nehls

PICTURE CREDITS

Cover photo by Rick Reinhard.

Photo on page 12, courtesy of the Child Welfare League of America, Inc. Photos on pages 32, 43, and 70 by Kathy Richland, courtesy of the Chicago Child Care Society. Photos on pages 26 and 111 courtesy of Adoptalk, Minneapolis, Minnesota. Photos on pages 62 and 64 are copyrighted by Rick Reinhard. The photo on page 52 is by Harry A. Trattner, courtesy of the Chicago Child Welfare League of America, Inc. Those on pages 56, 87, 121 and 125 are copyrighted by Bob Teitelbaum. Those on pages 20, 49, and 139 are reproduced with the permission of Christian Children's Fund, Inc., of Richmond, Virginia. Christian Children's Fund, it should be pointed out, is not an adoptive agency. Its nearly 300,000 sponsors in the United States and overseas contribute monthly to the support of individual needy children in the Third World countries. Thus, CCF sponsors assist these children to develop as healthy citizens within their own families, communities, and nations. Although the CCF children in the photographs are in no sense adopted by their sponsors, their basic problems -- hunger, malnutrition, lack of educational opportunities, and uncertain futures -- are similar to the problems of thousands of needy children in this country.

Prefaces

Preface to the Second Edition

In this second edition, we have devoted a chapter to an overview of the adoption literature of the last few years as it reflects on the findings of our study which were described in the first edition.

In addition, two aspects of the adoption experience have been considered more fully in this edition. First, the legal, ethical, and social issues concerning adoption are becoming increasingly more complex as evidenced by the difficulties many potential parents have in finding a child, and by the consequent proliferation of non-traditional ways of adopting, such as foreign adoptions, surrogate motherhood, and private adoptions.

The other aspect concerns the experiences of adolescent adoptees and their parents. A marked change in adoption practices has occurred over the past 20 to 30 years, and these changes continue to accelerate. We now have the opportunity to reflect on what adolescence is like for adoptees from other lands, for those racially different from their adoptive parents, and for those adopted in late childhood or during adolescence.

Foster care ends abruptly at 18, and often these young persons, due to many adverse life experiences, are at a disadvantage in negotiating the important transitions of late adolescence. Adoption, on the other hand, carries a different set of expectations: of continued parental involvement and support through the transitional years from adolescence to young adulthood, and of an evolving, mutually satisfying relationship between parents and grown children. The way the relationship unfolds during adolescence is therefore of crucial importance. The particular issues facing adoptive parents and their adolescent children deserve careful study and reflection. We hope that this second edition will make a contribution to understanding these facets of adoption.

Preface to the First Edition

Much has been written recently about bonding, the process that "attaches" mothers and their biological infants to each other, and several theories have evolved about how bonding occurs. But what about adopted children? How do such theories relate to them? What about bonding with a child who is adopted at an older age and who has already gone through some of the developmental stages deemed important to bonding? What happens when the child one adopts is handicapped or racially different from oneself? Since bonding involves others besides the adoptive parents and adopted child, how supportive are extended families and communities to adoptive parents, and how helpful are adoption agencies to them? How do foreign adoptions differ from domestic ones? Which factors lead to bonding and which to its opposite, distancing?

Our interest in these questions is both personal and professional. Both of us are nurses and concerned with assisting families to develop and grow, and one of us has adopted two children.

To gather the data on which this book is based, we tape-recorded sixty interviews with mothers and, using a questionnaire, received responses by mail from fifty-seven others. In addition, thirty-three adopted children over the age of ten completed a special children's questionnaire.

Why did we limit our study to mothers and children? Fathers are important, too! Primarily because we wanted to compare our data on adopted children to the current literature on bonding, and most of that literature deals with bonding between biological *mothers* and their children. What are some of the similarities of the adoptive situation to the biological one, and what are some of the differences?

We wrote this book because we wanted to share the results of our study (which are different from many descriptions of the adoptive experience) with parents, especially adoptive parents, and with professionals who work with adopted children and their families. Because parenting has many commonalities regardless of the characteristics of parent and child, the study will probably be of interest to all parents.

       — *Dorothy W. Smith*
       Laurie Nehls Sherwen

Acknowledgments

The contribution of the participants in the study was central, and we sincerely thank the mothers and children who generously shared their responses through interviews and questionnaires.

We thank the Charles and Johanna Busch Foundation, which provided funds for our project, and we extend special thanks to Mr. Francis Baran, of the Office of Research and Sponsored Programs, Rutgers University, for his timely and generous help and encouragement.

We are appreciative of Teuta Feinberg's contribution on pages 178 to 181 which demonstrates how adoptees feel about their adoptive mothers.

Bonnie Feldman and Janice Brzozowski did an excellent job of typing the manuscript.

We thank Helen Behnke for her interest in and support of the project.

Our colleagues at the College of Nursing who showed their interest and support are too numerous to mention individually. We thank them all for creating a climate which encourages research.

1

Adoption Diaries

Before describing our research and its results, we would like to share with you some diaries of "composite" adoption situations that we learned about during our study. While the situations described are real, we have supplied fictitious names and have altered other data, such as the children's ages and characteristics and descriptions of the adoptive families, so that the people involved cannot be identified.

We wrote this material after completing the study, distilling into it many of the concerns and needs which we heard voiced over and over again by participants in the study. We hope this chapter will give those of you who have adopted children a feeling of kinship as you recognize similarities to and differences from your own situation. For those who contemplate becoming adoptive parents, we offer it as a taste of what it has been like for some people. Your own situation may be entirely different. As is true throughout the book, we include not only ideal adoptive situations where all goes smoothly but also some difficult ones, because we believe that a great deal of literature on adoption makes light of the difficulties while somewhat sentimentally stressing the joys of instant parenthood. Our data suggest that the advantages of adoption for children and parents are very great, but that the path to achieving a close family tie with some children may be steep and rocky.

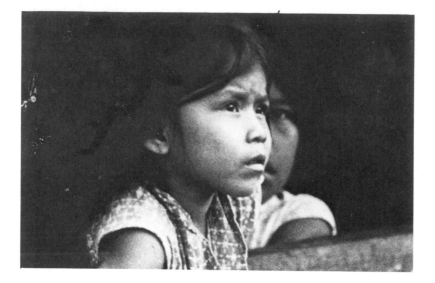

Maria

September 4:   It has happened. I got a call today saying a little girl in South America is now my little girl. There is much paperwork to be done, and we have to take a trip down there, but it is now a certainty. I think I'll tell the family and a few close friends. John is thrilled. I haven't told Jason yet. How does one tell a seven-year-old that he has an instant sister who is already five years old?

September 12:   Her picture arrived today. I find myself looking at it over and over each day, trying to sense what she is like. The picture is tiny and not very clear. It's all we have right now and very precious. John and I got a set of photos ready, showing our family and the house and our dog, and sent them down. We also included a description which we hope can be translated into Spanish for her, so she can begin thinking about us, too. Actually, I know almost nothing about her. She was abandoned as an infant and has lived in a orphanage since then.

October 9: I haven't bought anything for her, as I don't know her size and anyway I'm trying not to pin my hopes on it too much. It's a pretty risky venture after all. I'm trying to keep my mind off it till she's actually here, as it all seems so uncertain. No further word from the agency.

November 10: I sat down with Jason, showed him the picture, and explained about adoption and that he is going to have a sister. He was thrilled. Then he asked why he couldn't have a brother instead. I just said, "Because she's a girl." He laughed and so did I. Of course, this means he'll tell it all around the school, but I feel he needs time to prepare himself.

December 8: Getting ready for Christmas. I wonder if she'll be here by then. The uncertainty is beginning to get to both John and me, and it doesn't help when Jason and his friends keep asking about it. If John knew for sure when we'd be going, he could get time off from work. But he can't leave at the drop of a hat, especially since he just got promoted to manager of his division.

December 28: Christmas has come and gone and no Maria. John has found a friend willing to be her escort. Harry is retired and can go on short notice. We made out all the forms for an escort and sent them down. The uncertainty is growing all the time. I wonder if we really are going to have Maria. I'm glad we decided on the escort, as I can't very well leave Jason home and I don't want to take him out of school. I've heard of people who go down and plan to spend four days and end up spending four weeks to deal with all the red tape. We've done all we can. Just waiting now.

January 2: Harry went down four days ago to get Maria. If all goes as planned, he'll be at the airport at 9 P.M. tomorrow. I feel numb, then excited, then scared. I keep trying to be calm and also to keep my mind off it. I got her bed ready, but I think I'll wait till I see her size before shopping for clothers. My neighbor lent me a warm jacket and a few pairs of slacks and tops, some underwear, and a nightgown. We'll manage with that for now.

January 3:   John and Jason and I go to the airport. I feel as though my heart will burst from excitement. The jet pulls up, only a little late. The plane is festive looking: bright orange. Then I see Harry coming down the ramp, and right away a very pale, very little girl. She is stumbling along as though half asleep. Something is wrong with one of her eyes. Why didn't anyone tell us? I start feeling overwhelmed. Jason and John start putting on the warm clothes we brought for her, as it is snowing outside. I stand by feeling helpless and sort of in shock. Then I take Maria's hand while we walk out in the snow to the car. Once outside I begin to feel very protective of her. She puts her hand in mine very sleepily but also trustingly. She knows no one here, not even us. It is 11 o'clock by the time we get the children inside the house. Jason is exhausted and he has school tomorrow. He jumps into bed and is asleep instantly. I help Maria into the shower and wash her hair. It is strange: I had a feeling of wondering if she is a girl or a boy. I was relieved when I undressed her to see she is a girl. I check her head carefully. She had a treatment for lice before boarding the plane but I want to make sure... it looks O.K. I get her to bed, but when I turn out the big light she starts to scream a high-pitched continuous scream. I'm exhausted. I look at her and wonder how and why I ever let myself in for this. Jason wakes up in the next room and starts to cry. I feel I have deserted Jason in taking in this new child. John goes in to sit with Jason. The screaming continues. Finally Maria is exhausted and falls asleep. I wonder what happened to my maternal feelings for her. She is not at all the child I expected. I wonder what can be done for her eye. Her belly sticks out, but her arms and legs are as thin as toothpicks. Her hair is so thin I can see her scalp right through it.

January 4:   Maria grabs everyone's food and eats with her hands. She is terribly hungry. I am not prepared for the pandemonium at the table when Jason sees her grabbing his food. Except for meal times, Maria is quiet. I try out my limited Spanish. She and Jason begin communicating in a mixture of Spanish and English. Jason quickly becomes her interpreter. How do children do it?

January 7:   I take Maria to the doctor. As I assumed might happen, she has two kinds of intestinal parasites. I have to take stool specimens to the lab every week, and she is on two medications for parasites, and on vitamins and iron. I have an appointment with the eye specialist. Our doctor says he thinks the eye was damaged due to an infection. He says it might be serious. I will also take her to the dentist. I wonder what he will find. Trying not to feel discouraged. Very tired.

January 8: Maria started school today. There was some problem as she has just started her immunizations. She will go into kindergarten. Jason is very careful of her, takes her across the streets and sees that she buys her lunch. He is really knocking himself out to be helpful. Maria relates to Jason more than to anyone else.

January 12: What is happening? Maria has suddenly stopped being quiet. She runs in front of cars. She opens our car door and tries to get out while the car is moving. The locks on the back doors are supposed to be childproof, but she reaches out the window and releases them. She grabs matches and starts lighting up her shirt. Hits and bites Jason and takes his toys. Jason is slightly taller but no match for her aggressiveness. I feel desperate. Exhausted. Resentful, too, of not having more information before she came. The opthalmologist says her vision in that eye is only half what it should be—damage from infection. Nothing can be done.

January 14: John remains fairly calm. Why not? He's not here all day. When he's home, he helps me by holding Maria in her tantrums so she doesn't hurt Jason. When I'm alone, I can't hold her, as she wiggles away and then kicks me in the stomach. I've ended up sitting on her as a restraint. What sort of craziness is this? I can't figure out what is happening and what to do. I end each day exhausted. I scream at Jason all the time.

January 15: Maria's teacher says she is quiet in the classroom. Of course she knows no English yet. At least the teacher is not complaining. I don't tell her anything about what is happening at home.

January 22: Other mothers are complaining a lot about Maria. She doesn't get along well with other children. I've had several phone calls with complaints. What can I say? She is forbidden to play at most homes, so she wanders the streets more. At first people were interested. Now they just avoid her. Got a call from the teacher. Maria hit another child, gave him a bloody nose. She refused to mind. I had to go get her at the school, she was so disruptive. I spanked her once I got her home. The first time. She lost all reason, raced around the house screeching and throwing things. Dumped over my African violet and threw one of the fish out of the tank.

February 6: Today Jason came home from school, slammed down his school books, and said, "I'm not taking care of her anymore. I've had it." Jason's teacher says his work has fallen off badly, and he alternately daydreams and is irritable. He started wetting his bed again, after being over it for three years.

February 12: John comes home later and later from work. I feel left out. It's hard to get a sitter due to Maria's behavior, so we don't go out much. John thinks I take it all too seriously and too personally. I seem to be the only one who can't get away. Also, getting a shoe thrown at my head *is* personal.

March 10: A neighbor has a garage sale. Both Jason and Maria went and bought a few things. I was busy with the wash, so I didn't go until later. Maria bought me a gift from the sale and I thanked her. She almost never does anything nice and I felt touched. When I went to the sale, I saw a toy just like hers on the "for sale" table. I said, "Maria has a toy just like that." My neighbor said, "That is Maria's. She traded it for a gift." I got into the car and then I cried. It is the first sign of gentleness, tenderness, toward me. I think I haven't admitted to myself how much I miss some signs of affection from her. Maybe things will get better. I hug Maria when I get home and thank her again for the gift.

March 14: More trouble. Maria is going from door to door asking for money. I hit the ceiling. I scream. I send her to her room. Of course, I have to stay there with her, otherwise she won't stay in her room. Dinner is late again tonight. I make a secret promise to myself to find a way to get her into foster care. I don't say anything of this plan to John. He'll just give me a sermon. I can't take it anymore— the shame of it all, the complaints.

March 15: Well, I'll try it one more day. Not so much out of conviction but because I feel so exhausted and I don't want to make any more uproar.

March 16: I am thinking it over. Those other mothers who are calling me are saying how Maria is in trouble all the time and they don't want their kids in class with her. But I just talked to her teacher, and she didn't say Maria is doing so badly. In fact, she said she is doing better. I just don't know how to explain to people that you can't expect the same things from a child who has had no home and no parents as you can from the kids in the neighborhood. Of course those kids do better. Also, I come off looking like a bad mother. But I wonder how those mothers would handle Maria. I say as little as possible of what it is like at home, as the more I say, the more people will be turned off. I have a little glimmer of protectiveness for Maria. She's *my* kid and she's getting a bum rap.

April 10: Maria is now beginning to speak some English. It happened very suddenly. She has no accent. Amazing. What a smart little girl she is.

April 15: Today Maria started talking about her adoption. She was angry. She said, "You don't just go up to a girl and say, 'I want that one.'" We talked. I asked her if she felt she had no choice about coming here. She said yes. She now idealizes her orphanage. "We could have anything we wanted to eat, and as much as we wanted." I don't contradict her.

Maria is out playing kickball with some children across the street. This is the first time she has played and not come rushing back home, either because she isn't allowed to play or because a fight begins. Later she walks in like a conquering hero with a swagger and gets a cold drink. I feel proud of her.

April 16: Maria is stealing from my purse. A few dollars, and as much as forty dollars. Fortunately, I got the forty dollars back. But she did go buy ten dollars worth of junk candy. I'm surprised the storekeeper didn't question her having the ten dollar bill, but I suppose they have other things to think of. I have to hide my purse all the time.

May 14:   Maria and I go to the park alone. She is beaming and happy over the attention. I enjoy pushing her on the swing and playing with her. I feel as if she has just arrived. After all, I wanted her. I am happy.

June 2:   Maria still refuses to bathe and brush her teeth. A battle all the time. She has six cavities to fill. She has started running away. Even stays after dark. I worry, but she always comes back after a couple of hours. Once she returned with only one sneaker, as some big kids threw one of them in the bushes. I never found it. Her new ones, of course.

June 8:   Maria has started therapy. I hope the psychologist can help her. The expense is terrible, but time is going by, and while she makes some progress, she really does have to improve faster. John agrees that we have to do it. Jason is growing more sullen and cranky. I expect too much of him, wanting him to be good all the time as I can't cope with another child who isn't.

June 10:   I've decided to get a part-time job. I need to get out of the house and think of something else. Also, we can use the money. Joined an adoptive mothers' group. Several of the members know what I'm going through. It's a relief to be able to talk with them.

June 18:   Maria is talking more about the orphanage. How she was beaten and locked in a dark room. Some of the tales she tells are a mixture of fantasy and reality. She is very much preoccupied with hurting and being hurt, and also with death. Sometimes she wakes up screaming from her nightmares. Maria prays every night for her friends in the orphanage, and she is very gentle and sincere. She worries, knowing they are being whipped and that they are hungry, and that they may die. The death rate at the orphanage was high. She has seen children die. She seems so little to have gone through so much.

June 20:   I hurt my back. Maria is very tender and loving, putting out her little arms and saying, "Here, Mommy, I'll help you." She can be so sweet. She has rosy cheeks, her hair is thick and beautiful, shiny and black. She's all girl—very feminine. She is quite graceful. She used to walk like a little soldier—very stiff. Her eye will never look right, but it seems less noticeable now. She sees well enough, does well in her studies.

June 23: We joined a local pool. What a good idea. Jason and Maria both love it. They run and play and John and I have some time to ourselves. When I see her playing and swimming and being just a regular kid, I can hardly believe it. She is the picture of health, playful.

July 2: Today I held Maria on my lap and read to her. I hugged her and felt lucky to have her. She was very loving. We have so little of this, but perhaps more will come. The therapy is definitely helping her. She is much more aware of herself and her behavior and of others' reactions. Still wets her pants in daytime and her bed at night.

July 5: Today is my birthday and Maria gave me a bouquet of paper flowers she made. I am thrilled. She has fewer tantrums and the ones she has are shorter.

July 9: John and I are getting along better. He's home more, and I feel I get more support from him. Jason, finally, is having a more normal life as everything doesn't revolve around Maria and her behavior. The kids have a marvelous time at the pool and once home they're tired and go to sleep easily. I'm beginning to relax. In January, Maria will have been here a year. The other night while I was sitting on her bed getting her settled, she talked for the first time about her eye. She asked me what happened to it (apparently no one had told her), and she cried and asked why it had to be like that. I know she held that in for a long time.

July 15: Maria asked me about her bio parents. I have no information. She was in an orphanage most of her life. We talked about what she thinks and how she wishes they hadn't left her. She really has a lot to cope with. She has to keep up with the other children, no matter what has happened to her in the past. And she's doing pretty well at it, too.

July 21: Today Maria said she wished I'd had her since she was a baby. I wish so, too.

Kyung

Kyung is 13, a young girl of mixed Korean and American ancestry. Kyung has lived in an orphanage in Korea since she was six years old. Here is a portion of Kyung's diary.

February 2:   A lawyer came here to see me and asked if I would like to be adopted. I was surprised. I just figured I'd be here about two more years and then try to get a job. Maybe I could get a job here at the orphanage. I've known other girls who have done that. I didn't know what to say. I just said yes. I had to say something. I'm not sure what it all means.

February 3:   I asked the orphanage director what adoption is and she explained. She also told me there is a family in the United States who would like to adopt me. She said it would give me a chance for a better life. She explained things I already know: that it will be hard for me here in Korea, because I am mixed Korean-American, and because I don't have parents to help me. I guess she's right. I'll miss all my friends, though, and I don't know any English. I asked if she knew any more about the family who want to adopt me, but she doesn't know any more than that. I'd like to have a picture or a letter from them. I just have to wait now.

February 18: My orphanage director came to tell me I now have a passport to go to the United States. I will travel by plane. There will be a stewardess on the plane who will care for us during the trip. My family will meet me at the airport. She gave me a pretty new dress to take with me—one that some rich people gave for the children here. I like the dress, but I'm confused and frightened. I want to go, but I also don't want to go. My friends wish they could be adopted, too. If just one of my friends could come with me, I'd feel better.

February 20: I wonder if I will have a pony. I've heard that all children in the United States have ponies.

February 26: Tomorrow I leave. I cry a lot, especially at night. I probably will never come back to see my friends again. Sometimes I feel excited. Maybe it will be wonderful.

March 2: So much has happened the last few days. The flight was very long. I slept some on the plane, and we had a lot to eat. There were six other children from Korea on the plane, and that helped. At least I wasn't alone. The stewardess was nice. She showed us games to play. One girl got sick to her stomach, but I didn't. My new parents were at the airport. There was a big crowd all around. The stewardess stayed with us till we had all found our parents. Lots of noise and I couldn't understand a word anyone said. My parents hugged me. I can't describe my feelings, except that I was so tired and so scared, and I was glad that at least they were there. I worried: what if no one meets me?

March 5: I am starting to feel more like myself. I have been waking up when everyone else is sleeping, and getting hungry at night. The stewardess warned me that I might feel this way because the time is different here from Korea. I have a whole room to sleep in all alone. I've never slept in a room alone before. I don't want to act like a baby, so I don't let on I'm afraid to be alone at night. The food is strange, but I can have as much as I want. There is no fighting over food, and I don't have to hide any as I can just go get some when I want it.

My new mother seems nice but she is very different from people in Korea. My father leaves the house every morning and comes home in the evening, but my mother stays here with me. I am disappointed at not having brothers and sisters. I don't like being the only child here. There is really no one my age at all. I can't understand much of anything except gestures. My mother has a dictionary of Korean and English words. She points to the Korean words when she has to explain something. We are beginning to laugh together as we work with the dictionary. That is how she told me I'll start school next week.

March 6:   My mother took me to a store, and I now have a new pair of jeans, something I've always wanted. I got shoes and sneakers and dresses and skirts, underwear, a coat, everything. I got so excited. It was the first time I felt relaxed with my mother. She seemed so happy that I was happy. We laughed a lot and went to a restaurant afterward. Later I put on my new clothes to show my father. He smiled and gave me a kiss. I don't know him very well at all.

March 8:   I've met some of my parents' friends and some neighbors. It is strange. Everyone acts as though this is where I'm supposed to be and as though this is my home. I don't feel that way. I feel like a stranger and a visitor. I dream at night, always about my friends in Korea. Everyone here seems to expect me to be happy and I'm really not. I'm homesick and lonely. Tonight my mother sat on the edge of my bed when I was ready to sleep, and all of a sudden she put her arms around me and hugged me close. I started to cry. First time I've done it where others could see me. She just held me a long time, and then I saw she was crying, too. Maybe she knows I'm not very happy and maybe she is scared, too.

March 12:   My first day at school. Noise and confusion. I am used to a small class at the orphanage, where all the girls go together. We had class only in the morning, and in the afternoon we did work, like cleaning and helping with the younger children. This school lasted all day. Boys and girls. People moving from one class to another every hour. One girl had been asked to sit with me, eat with me, and take me to classes. Otherwise I wouldn't have known what to do. No one speaks Korean. I can't see how this is going to work out at all, and today I will tell my mother to please help me get back to Korea.

March 20:   I notice that my mother now leaves in the morning when I leave for school. She has a job. She gets home a little while after I do. I have the key to the house. I go in and wait for her. It is only half an hour or so till she comes, and I watch the TV while I wait. My parents are quite rich. A color TV, a dishwasher, machines for washing and drying clothes, a big house. Everyone around here seems rich. They act very used to all this, and I suppose they are. My mother tells me to put my clothes I've worn into a bin every night. Then they get washed. I used to wash only my underwear that often.

March 25:   I have to be in a special class at school. That way I can catch up and also learn English. I wish I could have stayed with Mary, the girl who took me around that first day, but I can't. Anyway she invited me to her house after school tomorrow. I have a special teacher helping me with English.

March 27:   I had a good time at Mary's house. My mother seemed happy too that I went. It gives her some time for herself I suppose. There is going to be a week's vacation next week, and my mother is talking to me about how I may spend my time. She and my father will be working I can visit Mary sometimes. I can study my English, watch TV. It sounds boring.

April 15:   Today my mother and father and I went to the city. We saw a play and went out to dinner. It was a thrill. I've never been in a theater before, and I never ate in a restaurant till I came here.

April 19:   I met Donna, who lives near us. She came over Saturday afternoon. Mother gave me money and Donna and I went to a skating rink. I never skated before, but it was fun. I'm beginning to understand some of what people say to me, and I find I understand gestures better than I used to.

April 21: I haven't done any cleaning since I left Korea. No laundry either. My mother doesn't ask me to help, and so I don't. But it doesn't seem natural. She goes ahead and does everything. She even mends my clothes. I used to take care of my own clothes and help the younger girls too. I'm going to surprise mother and offer to help.

April 22: That was the right thing to do. My mother was happy and said thank you. We cleared up the dishes after dinner and I helped by putting laundry into the machine. Mother showed me how to work it.

May 1: Today while mother and I were clearing away the dinner dishes I began telling her something about my life in Korea. She and I can understand each other fairly well now by using sign language and some words we both understand. She seemed interested in what I was telling her. She got a cup of tea, and we sat in the kitchen quite awhile together.

May 3: Some boys at school hollered at me, calling me Chinese. Then a girl started calling me dumb because I go to a special class. When I went home I was angry. I banged things in my room, threw my books. I hate those kids. My mother came in and yelled at me—the first time she has done that. I yelled back, "I hate you. I wish I were back in Korea." I was sorry later. She and I have been very polite with each other all this time. I can't be polite all the time anymore. Later at dinner she was over being angry and so was I. We talked about what happened at school, and she had some ideas about what I could say back to those kids.

May 5: My English teacher says I am doing very well. I can speak in short sentences and I know a lot of English words. People tell me I have an accent though. I've been doing a lot of different things that I never did in Korea, like going to movies and skating. Donna and Mary are both very nice. I sent a letter back to my orphanage with a picture of me in my new jeans. I hope they will write back.

May 8: My father and I went to a baseball game. The first time he and I did something together. As they say in English, he is neat. On the way home, we passed through a big city and I saw very poor

people and really poor little kids playing in the street. All of a sudden I felt very sad. I know what it feels like to be poor and I went hungry a lot. I cried, and at first my father didn't understand, but when I explained he did understand. He put his arm around me and said, "Well, now you are not poor any more." I would like to have stopped to help those people but we just went on by. Somehow it doesn't seem right that I got out of the orphanage but there are still kids there who are my friends.

May 15:   School will soon be over. We will be going away to the beach for two weeks when my father and mother have their vacations. I've never been anywhere really except the orphanage. It sounds great. I'm taking swimming lessons at the Y. At first I was scared of the deep water, but now I love it. Yesterday we all went to the circus.

June 2:   A letter came today from Korea, from my orphanage. Several of my friends wrote notes on the letter, and the director sent me a greeting also. I had a very strange feeling. I remember it all, but I know I've changed a lot since I was there. I'm quite different. I hope I am not getting fresh like some American kids. When I first came here I couldn't believe the way they talked to their teachers. But now I realize that the ways people act are different here. Also, only some kids are fresh. Most of them are nice.

June 18:   Mother and I went to a picnic for adopted children and their parents. That was some experience. I guess I thought most adopted children in the U.S.A. are Korean. There were regular American kids, some of them white, some black. I met some kids from Korea, Vietnam, and Colombia. We sure were a mixture. On the way home I asked my mother, "Are you sure all those kids were adopted?" She said yes. So I'm not such an oddball after all. That group will have other parties and trips and we plan to go.

June 23:   School is over. And I realize that most of the time now I feel happy. I just feel good in a way I never did before. I guess I missed having parents and a home, even though at the time I wouldn't have thought of it that way since the orphanage seemed like my home. I still miss my old ways sometimes, but mostly I'm happy. I was lucky. I got really neat parents.

Margaret

December 1:   I hear the news from the social worker. I'm going
to be a mother and a single one at that. I wonder if I can manage. I
have my child's picture. A six-year-old girl. I hope she can come for
Christmas. I don't believe it. After four years of waiting.

December 12:   The social worker says no, best for her to stay
with her foster family over Christmas. Well, she'll be here soon. I'll
send her a gift marked from Santa Claus.

January 4:   I drove three hours each way, and I saw her. She is
part Korean and part American in ancestry. I felt very strange. Alternately thrilled and numb. I'm glad I can take it a bit gradually. I
didn't tell anyone except Cynthia. It could still fall through.

January 15:   My second visit. The next time, my daughter
Margaret comes home with me. I've been afraid to buy anything
for her, for fear of jinxing it. But I know her size is a four, and tomorrow I'm going clothes shopping. She seems like such a happy, sunny
little girl. I wonder if she realizes she's really coming to live with me.
I know she's been prepared, but how much does a small child take in
of the explanation?

January 22: We made it. She's here. She loved the long car ride but fell apart once she arrived. All the careful preparation, the visits and pictures, seem to be for nothing. She runs through the house screaming. She wets herself constantly. She won't eat. Won't dress. I don't know what to do. All she wants is to sit in front of the TV. I guess that's all that's familiar. She sits right close to it as though it is her mother. I think I better not try to stop her from doing it now.

January 24: A visit to the doctor. Margaret is small but otherwise healthy.

January 25: I take Margaret to school. She seems very tiny to go to that big school. I found someone to care for her after school— a woman who has a girl Margaret's age and a younger girl, too. Also a playroom and a big yard. I'm glad, as Margaret needs playmates.

January 28: Margaret is starting to eat. Thank goodness. She talked with her foster mother on the phone. She really brightened after the phone call.

January 30: Today Margaret was all upset. Crying. Hard for me to understand her. I finally realized she fears that her social worker does not know where she is. Her social worker is the most important person to her. I'll ask the social worker to contact Margaret directly, to show she does know where she is.

February 6: When I give Margaret dolls to play with she is not interested, and sometimes she pushes them angrily away. She is full of questions about where babies come from. It is as though she has been saving up these questions and now has someone to ask. She still wets the bed and her pants but is growing fast.

February 9: This evening Margaret wanted me to read her the "life story" book which her social worker made for her. We talked about her foster mother and the other foster children. She misses them terribly. She has talked with them on the phone a few times and that seems to help. When she is in the tub I hear her talking and when I go in she tells me she is talking to her "playmates." I started to worry. Then I realized they are imaginary playmates. She must be lonely here.

February 19: Margaret seems happier most of the time. She brags about me to her friends even though she often balks at my demands, such as about eating, washing, and dressing. I heard from Margaret's teacher that she tells the other children she has six brothers and six sisters. It is really a big change for her not to have all those foster children around.

March 3:   Margaret and I took our first trip together. I had to go to a meeting. The hotel assured me that they have sitters. (Later I found out this is a very expensive arrangement.) Margaret got sick. I was up all of one night. Margaret vomited all over my bed, as she had come into my bed when she did not feel well. I took her to a doctor next day: fever, coughing, vomiting. I missed some of the really good meetings. But we had some good moments, too. She loved the plane ride.

March 14:   Margaret talks of her bio mother and wants to meet her. I explained that this may be possible later but not now. She tells me what she imagines her bio mother is like. I am trying to think of a way to explain to a six year old why she cannot see her bio mother. I settle for something to the effect that her bio mother found she could not keep her, and that because she loved her she arranged for her to be adopted. It was the best I could do I have the feeling she's kept many of these questions to herself for a long time.

March 18:   The social worker from the agency near here is coming for a visit today. Margaret is all upset. Her teacher said she refused to do anything at school. This morning she told me a story about a dog who used to live at the foster home, who got put out because he messed on the rug. I assured her no one will put her out of here. I felt torn about what to say to the social worker. After all, the main reason she has come is to see if it is all right for Margaret to stay here. Things are rocky, but I tried to emphasize the positive.

March 21:   Margaret came home from school crying. The other children are teasing her, calling her "Chink." She thinks there's something wrong with her. I try to explain but she really doesn't understand. I decide on a treat. We go to dinner at McDonald's and she is all smiles again.

March 30:   The teacher says Margaret is having a lot of trouble with school work. She has never colored pictures and doesn't know how. She is not ready to read. She often just sits and watches the other children. Apparently she has spent a great deal of her life in front of a TV set. I find I can't push her too much. She just cries when I turn the TV off. She grows, it's amazing. Two pairs of shoes already.

April 6:   Margaret is sick again. I found someone at the last minute, after making about six phone calls, but I feel uneasy leaving her. She's sick a lot—all minor things—and I do have to get to work. I never figured on all these colds and stomach upsets. We have some good times, though. I love to take her out to plays and concerts and zoos and to the circus.

May 11:   A glorious warm day. I lay down on a blanket in the sun in the backyard. Margaret was playing near me. Then Margaret took a blanket, lay down beside me, rolled herself inside the blanket, and came out at the bottom of her rolled-up blanket. I was lazily inattentive and then she did it again. All of a sudden I caught on. I asked her what she was doing. She said, "I'm a baby being born. I'm being born your baby, Mommy." I was so thunderstruck I didn't know what to say. I just said something about her wanting to be my baby, and she said yes. Later when I was inside getting supper, I wondered if I was good enough, secure enough, to take all this responsibility. Margaret is adopting me as her mother.

June 18:   Margaret is starting day camp. She'll have other children to play with. She is very lonely and a lot of people in the neighborhood have gone away on vacation, so there just is no one to play with. Also, I can't stand the whining.

June 20:   I'm thinking about what it is like to be a mother. Didn't have time to think before. Now that school is out I feel relieved, because some of my stress had to do with helping Margaret meet demands she was not ready to meet. Demands which would be minor for the average child were major ones for her, and I felt I was always trying to buy time for her to catch up. The camp presents few demands. She goes for fun, she likes it, and that is super. My day's work is over at 4:30 and I used to relax then. Now I go into high gear all over again as soon as I get home, fixing dinner, getting Margaret to eat, bathe, and brush her teeth. She still balks, but not quite as much as at first. I haven't been away from her at all as she is so small and clinging. But this summer I'm going to take a weekend for myself. The sitter says she can sleep there one night. I'll present it as a "sleepover" but will also mention I'll be away one night, so as not to trick her.

June 28:   Margaret takes a van to day camp. I sit out on the front steps with her waiting for her van to come. She is a little bundle of energy, clutching her swim suit, towel, and sandwich. She is so eager, she seems like a little time bomb. She bounds into the van and waves goodbye merrily. Others don't know all the neglect she's had. She goes off with the other children, she manages; she's a plucky little girl.

July 2:   It's strange, but as soon as Margaret came, my friends who have children treated me like a "mother among mothers" right away. It was as though suddenly I knew all about kids' birthday parties, car pools and all that. I don't, but I'm learning fast. Today I took Margaret to a birthday party which was also a swim party.

July 8:   I'm relieved not to have all the daily contact with the sitter and the mothers of children at the school. Margaret goes to camp in the van and gets dropped off at home when camp is over. I'm home just before she returns. It's a big relief not to be trying to keep up with the "other mothers," most of whom do not work except for their housework. I do that on top of a full-time job, and it bores me and annoys me to hear about their fancy cooking and housekeeping. I feel I should be doing it too. I have so little time, and when I do have time I like to go out and have a good time with Margaret, and not be stuck in the kitchen.

We go to a pool and to a park where they have rides for kids. She loves it and it's fun for me, too. Sometimes I find people giving me advice and butting in in a way I'm sure they wouldn't if I were married. It's as though they think I'm not capable or something. On the other hand, most people treat me as very capable. Oh, the heck with all this thinking. Time to get ready to take Margaret to the pool. She's learning to swim.

July 12: Margaret and I are going to visit friends at the beach. I find I am drawing closer to my friends who have small children. It's good for me to be around them and their kids—gives me some perspective. It's easy to think all problems are due to adoption. Some of the problems are just typical of kids a certain age, and I need to see that. Margaret quickly finds her niche among the children at such get togethers, and I have time with my friends. Sometimes I miss my lazy weekends. Margaret used to wake me at 5 A.M. every day, including Sunday. When I asked her why, she said, "I want to make sure you are alive." Now she doesn't wake me till six. She goes to bed easily. I rock her and sing to her. She loves it. Also, that is the best part of my day. I sit there in her room with the night light on and relax. I can see the pretty things I've bought for her. I feel very peaceful then, which is just about the only time all day that I stop and relax. I've been so tired lately that I go to bed by 9:30.

July 20: It's hard to believe Margaret isn't legally mine. I feel no doubt about being her mother. At first, I was glad for the year's trial period. But now I'm eager for it to be settled. Have to wait till January, when we go to court and see the judge. I wondered if I should tell Margaret about the trial period and I decided not to. It would only add insecurity. A few days before we go to court I'll explain it as a ceremony to celebrate and make definite that we are mother and daughter.

August 1: Margaret is changing. She used to run up to everyone. Didn't matter that they were strangers. She treated everyone alike. I understood it but it also annoyed me. Here I was her mother but she treated me no differently than some stranger at the airport. Sometimes it was embarrassing. This behavior is lessening. She cried today in a very different way than before. It used to be a whiny, sort of mechanical, demanding cry. Today she cried in a very wholehearted way, saying "I want my mommy." I knew that was me all right. She now loves to play with her dolls.

August 5: I've found a group of single adoptive parents and joined. It feels good to talk to parents who aren't always discussing how they spend three hours decorating cakes, or how they are sewing drapes. The kids were all ages from infants to about 16, and all colors and nationalities. A lot of the talk was about making ends meet, in terms of time and money. The parents and kids seemed happy. It wasn't at all the stereotype of the downtrodden helpless single mother. Those women were active and managing. There were three fathers there, too. Margaret had a fine time. She met two girls from Korea. I am always amazed at how fast children establish their own networks.

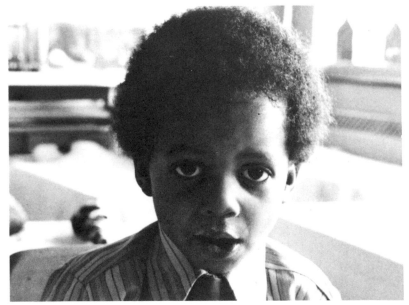

John

September 2: We've heard of a five-year-old boy waiting for adoption. He's black and white mixed ancestry. Bill and I have been wanting a baby. We've imagined a baby who looks like us. I wonder if we should get involved in this. I'm more and more interested. I don't understand our good fortune. I know others who have been waiting for years. We just completed our home study six months ago.

September 3: Bill and I are going to visit him at the foster home tomorrow. His name is John. I have no picture. I don't know what to expect. The social worker will go with us.

September 5:   I wanted to take him right home the minute I saw him. Bill was as ready as I. There he stood, big, healthy, with beautiful round big brown eyes, brown curls, and pretty brown skin. And a smile that could melt a heart of stone. It was all settled, as far as we were concerned, at that first meeting. The social worker said it will take a week to get all the papers in order. She also said that even though John is very young he needs some preparation for the move. She will talk to him about it. She has some stories for young children which she believes will help him understand. We can visit him again in a few days. We'll take him a toy and play with him. The social worker said, as we were leaving, "Even though his ancestry is both black and white, people will deal with him as a black child. You need to realize that and consider it thoughtfully."

September 8:   I worried how my mother and brother would react. They are full of excitement and can't wait to see John. I guess I really knew they'd react this way. I wondered what I would do if they were against it, and yet I knew what I would do. I would go ahead anyway, but it would have been hard.

September 15:   He's here. It all happened so fast. I am still working on getting his room ready. He seems quite contented, playing with his toys. I'm wondering if he'll be upset later. He'll miss his foster mother. Tonight after I got him washed and into bed I just sat and looked at him. So beautiful, and so peaceful looking in his sleep. Then suddenly I felt afraid. I looked at him and I thought, "What have I done? Does he belong here?" I felt panicky for a minute. I went downstairs and talked to Bill. He says it's natural to feel that way. After all he's not a baby anymore. And he's of different race. Is it all right?

September 20:   I haven't had any more qualms. It was just a sudden flash. Now I feel it is so right. John is eating well, and he sleeps through the night. Such a secure, friendly, outgoing child. He cried for his foster mother twice at night. She must have been good for him, and to him. He talked with her on the phone, and tomorrow we'll visit her. I think he needs to see her and know she is alive and still cares about him. Who knows what he's imagining—perhaps that she is sick, or dead, or that she doesn't love him anymore.

September 23:   The visit helped. John ran to his foster mother; she held him. We both explained to him again about adoption, stressing that she cares about him and will enjoy hearing from him. He left very calmly with me. I wanted to ask what he was thinking, but couldn't find a way. But I took his hand, and he held it extra tightly as we left. I think he understands, as well as a five year old can, that he's my son now.

September 26:   John is unusually bright. Just as quick as can be. Now that he is getting settled here I must enroll him in kindergarten. The pediatrician says he is in the upper quartile for height and weight. He's very healthy.

October 1:   I finally got up my nerve and asked the social worker how we got a child so fast when others wait so long. She said John had been released for adoption and that another couple had planned to adopt him. Then they decided they couldn't cope with the racial issue, and they backed out. She called us. I felt suddenly sad for those other people. But I quickly put the thought aside. We are John's lucky parents. Bill's family are coming to visit next month, from Florida. We sent them John's picture.

October 18:   I took John to school for his first day. He didn't want me to leave, so I stayed an hour. Actually he was there only two hours by himself. That was enough for the first day. He was happy and bubbly on the way home. He had painted a picture. I forgot to mention to the teacher that he is adopted and I guess the principal forgot too. I laughed to myself when she looked kind of startled, seeing us together. I just said, "He's adopted." No big deal. She seemed to like John.

October 20:   John is beginning to make friends. He was playing with a group of other boys. They all went in one of the boy's homes. John came home crying. He wasn't allowed in. I asked why and he said, "Because Billy's father was mugged once." Obviously he was repeating an explanation he had just heard. I doubt he knew what mugged meant. But he knew he was excluded. My first reaction was to go pound their door down and get into a "How dare you" discussion. Decided the best thing for John is not to have a big flap. He needs friends, he's making them, and all the neighbors except that one family are supportive and interested. This experience has left me shaken. These things do occur. John will not be immune, and neither will we.

October 26: John is getting along just fine at school. He loves it, and he does well. There are two other non-white children: one is black, and the other is Korean. The children seem to get along well together. The other evening John announced, seemingly out of the blue, that he is white, and that his foster mother says white is best. I said, "No, John, you are mixed black and white. Your father was black, and your mother was white..." He looked puzzled. I guess no one had told him this. I turned to our dog who is black and white and said, "See, Rover is black and white. Both colors. She is beautiful." We ended up playing with Rover. I know he doesn't understand and that the analogy to the dog doesn't help, but I didn't see how to explain it to him. I was stunned that he is already into "white is best."

November 6: Bill's family came for the weekend. They just hugged John close, said how beautiful he is. They brought him a big truck, and also a boy doll which is a little darker in skin color than John. I saw Bill start to set the doll aside. (Dolls are for girls in his view.) I quickly put it back where John could play with it. John likes both toys and ended up with the doll in the driver's seat of the truck.

November 16: John and I went to McDonald's for supper. Bill is working late tonight. There was a mixed race family at the table next to us. It occurred to me that now we are a mixed family too. We smiled at one another, and the children started to play. They had three children. I realized I had my chance to explain mixed ancestry to John. When we left the restaurant I explained to John that he had a parent of each race, just as those children did. One child had looked a lot like John. I saw John smile—he understood. I feel as though my own horizons are broadening very fast. It felt very good to be with that family.

November 28: Thanksgiving is over. Soon it will be Christmas. We are going to Florida to visit Bill's family. Christmas means a lot more now that we have John. I am busy buying toys. Spending too much. By next year I will be sensible. I love seeing Bill so happy. "My son," he keeps saying. We are having a very easy time with

John. He is loving, playful, and does well in school. I am proud of him.

January 6:   Travelling with John is great. He loves it. He and I travelled alone as Bill couldn't spend that much time away from work. He had four days, but John and I had a week to spend with Bill's family in Florida. Whenever I was struggling with a bag plus tending John I suddenly got help. The people who helped were black. I realized that John and I were being included in a network of mutual help. It gave me a lot to think about. I wonder who John will marry. More to the point, I wonder if, when John is grown up, we'll still be "included" as his parents. How will he and his friends and his family feel about us then? It seems foolish to worry. I am experiencing so much that is positive.

February 8:   Snow season. John is learning to ice skate, and I took him to a park where he can use his sled. Took two of his friends along. Motherhood is really strenuous. I was glad to drop off the other two kids at their homes. That left me with only one soaking wet child to dry, warm and tend. John is growing fast.

March 18:   It is time to think about summer. There's a day camp here where the enrollment is about half black and half white. Bill and I have decided to send John, although it's very expensive. We think John needs to have more black friends, and it is a really good camp. We are going to get a membership at a swim club, too. We can all go on outings easily and often.

April 19:   I went to apply for the swim club. Had to go pick up the forms. I don't believe what happened. I am still numb. John trotted in beside me as he always does. The manager looked first at me, then at John. His face got an angry red. He said, "Your don't expect me to take *that*, do you?" looking at John. I was so enraged, I grabbed John and got in the car. I sat there shaking for a minute or so. John said, "What's the matter, Mommy, won't we go to the pool?" I managed to say, "No." We drove home in silence. I don't think John understood what had happened, but he knew I was upset. I feel I handled the whole thing badly. Now that I'm home I can think of a hundred things to say to that man. I told John we would find another pool, which we did.

May 21: Soon school will be over. John has done really well. We've had two visits from our social worker, which went well. In September the adoption will be final. I'll be glad when it's all settled.

June 28: John is very happy at camp, learning to swim. It is a more mixed group racially and I think that is really good. We mothers chat while waiting for our children when the day is over. I'm beginning to feel like an old hand at motherhood already. One thing is for sure. There is no way I can say John looks like me, and the fact of adoption is clear. Maybe that has advantages. I used to feel I had to explain all the time that he's adopted. Now it all seems so natural, I just say he's my son. When necessary, I say he's adopted, but I find that a lot of explaining isn't necessary. We've met a black family through the camp. Bill and I like the parents and Timmy has become John's best friend. When John is a little older we may transfer him to a parochial school which has an enrollment of about one-third black children.

Jason

April 8: After six years of waiting I'm going to be a mother. Tomorrow! I thought I would faint when I got the call at work. I phoned Ted right away at his office. He was stunned, then thrilled.

A baby boy. He's of Scotch-Irish ancestry like us, and as far as I know, in perfect health. Three days old. We have to pick him up tomorrow. My neighbor has a six month old and has plenty of baby clothes. I have so much to do and so little time! I hope that she will let me borrow a few clothes. I'm sure she will. I don't even have a crib. I don't want to buy just any old thing in a rush. I know. I have that antique cradle my grandfather made that I've used just to look pretty by the fireplace. Today I'll get crib sheets and blankets, plastic sheets, diapers. Formula. Oh, yes, bottles. I better make a list so I can stop on my way home. I must think of the things I really must have. There will be time on Saturday to do the main shopping. My sister will care for him on Saturday while we are out. We can get a really good crib, a dresser, clothes. I'll think of all that later. I don't have time to notice how I feel. Just breathless. We waited so long. I just figured nothing would ever come of our application. Also, I know I could have done it more quickly, but I wanted a baby, and a baby as near like one I could give birth to as possible.

April 9:   Ted took the day off but he had trouble about it as he couldn't give any notice. There's a big meeting he was supposed to attend. Finally he just told his boss, "Well, if my wife were giving birth you wouldn't even question my absence. This is the day my son arrives, and I'm going to be there." I sure hope the boss doesn't take it out on him later. He's up for promotion. But Ted was right, and I was proud of him for standing up for himself. We are due at the agency at 10:30 this morning.

April 10:   I am so tired, but happy. When we got to the agency the social worker brought our baby right to us. A beautiful baby boy! Round pink little face. I held him and at that moment he was mine. That was it. Then Ted held him. We both laughed and cried a little too. Something funny did happen that bothered me a little, and was like a black cloud on this beautiful day. I undressed him to put our own clothes on him. It seemed a little silly, but I felt I would really make him mine if I got rid of all remnants of his past life. I looked at his stomach, and there was the little black cord that had attached him to his biological mother! It made me feel a little strange, to think of that "link" to another mother still being present on my baby. I couldn't wait for it to fall off—irrational, but that's how I felt! Thank Heavens we had been at the agency before and knew the social worker. But I couldn't wait to get out of there and get the baby home. I was so tense. I felt that at any moment some paper would be found saying he was not legally free for adoption. Once I got home I just sat and held him and looked at him. The most beautiful baby I ever saw. Ted is as crazy about him as I am. Then we tucked him into the cradle and I rocked him while he slept. I just felt he knew he was home. I can't explain it, but I felt he knew. I was up three times to him during the night and today I feel wrung out.

April 13: We got the crib, the dresser, the clothes, some toys. Fortunately, we could charge most of it. I'm taking a leave of absence from work, although I probably won't return until Jason goes to school. I tried to talk my boss into a "maternity leave" period with pay, but he did not seem too receptive—maybe because the company is small and can't afford it. We sure will miss my salary, especially since there are three of us now. Yesterday the pediatrician examined Jason and says he is fine and healthy. He takes his formula well. Usually wakes and cries twice during the night. We are fixing up his room. When Ted has his summer vacation he's going to put some cute wallpaper on the walls. My first job at home was to clear out some Christmas ornaments and sewing things I had stored in the spare room. It looks like a nursery already. The cradle is back by the fireplace. I am starting to try to nap in the afternoon while he's sleeping. Looks like I'll be getting up at night for awhile.

April 15: I wonder if all new mothers feel so exhausted! I never realized that such a little baby could cause so much work! Jason is adorable, though, and I can't imagine our life without him. I wish I could breastfeed him. I feel so close to him when I give him his bottle—I wonder what I'm missing. I'm jealous of my breastfeeding friends!

April 17:   Jason had a bad night—seemed colicky, and was spitting up his formula. I really didn't know what to do for him. Ted and I were so scared! The baby just screamed and all I could do was hold him and cry along with him. At about five in the morning I started feeling angry, which is a terrible thing to feel toward a baby. But I get so tired. I also feel like a drudge a lot of the time. Neither Ted nor I got any sleep last night. I hope Ted's tiredness doesn't affect his work too much. His boss is still considering his promotion and, boy, do we need the increased income now!

April 20:   Jason has been fine for the last two days. I called the pediatrician in the morning after that terrible night, and he acted like I was a hysterical mother! I was rather insulted. How do I know what's serious and what's not? Nobody ever taught me what it's really like to be a mother! Oh, yes—some good news! Ted got his promotion. Hooray!

April 27:   We are really a family! It hasn't even been a month, and Jason has made such a change in our lives. The best part of the week for us is Sunday morning. Then we all stay in our bed together until at least 10 A.M. Ted and I hold Jason across our laps and make up stories about him—what he'll look like when he gets older, how he'll do in school, how he'll play soccer, what kind of mother-in-law I'll make when he (horrors!) marries some woman. I wonder what he thinks of it all. He seems to enjoy it and enter right into our game.

April 28:   I had a nightmare last night. I dreamed that Jason's biological mother came to our house, demanding to have him back. I remember grabbing him up into my arms and running away, screaming, "You can't have him back!" I woke up crying and got Ted all upset. I guess I've been too scared to give any thought to Jason's biological mother. I told the social worker that I didn't want to know anything about her. The only thing I know is that she was very young—only fifteen. What will happen if she changes her mind when she gets older? Can there be any legal recourse for her after we legally adopt Jason? Questions, questions. I remember awful stories in the newspaper. I don't even want to think about it!

May 1: Jason will be baptized on Sunday. Ted's family is not coming but my parents and my sister will be there. When Ted said his folks weren't coming, I couldn't believe it. I can see Ted is hurt. What can we do? They just feel Jason isn't their grandson. We'll have a family dinner afterward. I'm busy getting ready.

May 12: The social worker called today to make an appointment for a visit. At first I felt startled. I was really starting to feel Jason is ours and forget about that awful dream. When she called I realized he isn't legally ours yet. We have to wait a whole year for the legal adoption. I must try to be polite and cooperative when she comes. She reminds me that Jason isn't fully ours yet; I don't want the visit.

May 18: The visit with the social worker went well. I saw her eyes light up when I showed her his room. It really is pretty. And Jason is the picture of a healthy, happy baby. The social worker suggested an adoptive mothers' group. I felt miffed but I hope I didn't show it. Jason is my baby. I don't want to hear about adoption anymore. I have no reason to tell anyone he's adopted, except people I know really well. Everyone says he looks a lot like me.

May 20: I am fuming mad! I read an article in the newspaper that actually sympathized with a biological mother who gave up her baby and then tried to search for him. In the same article, I read about a 14-year-old adopted girl who wanted her adoption records opened so she could find the woman whom she called "her *real* mother!" What about the adoptive parents? Don't they have feelings? I think I'd leave the state if Jason's biological mother ever tried to enter our lives! The adoption triangle—what nonsense! I wonder if other adoptive mothers feel the same way I do. Perhaps I should think about that group the social worker mentioned. Will talk to Ted about it.

May 31: I think I'll go to that adoptive mothers' group to see what it is like. I'm really starting to feel a need for someone to talk to who is in the same situation as Ted and I. The social worker left me the name of the person to call. I can take Jason along, which is good.

June 3: I was interested in the mothers' group. They were talking about what and when to tell children about adoption. There will be a guest speaker at the next meeting who has done some research on that topic. I also talked to two other mothers who live close to me about "open records." They both said they felt like me at first, but are starting to feel better about it. One of the mothers even said that she now feels so close to her child that she could even help her daughter search for the biological mother when and if she wants to.

June 8: Ted's parents are coming over. His mother sounded kind of sheepish on the phone. They really hurt us, but on the other hand I don't want a rift in the family. They're coming for Sunday dinner. I guess nothing is easy or uncomplicated. Anyway, Jason is surely worth it all!

A Single Parent's Story

To conclude this chapter, here is a brief description, written by an adoptive mother, of what it is like to become the single parent of a little girl adopted at age five and a half.

What is it like, bonding with an older child? Initially, it is like being with a stranger. Everything is new, unknown; there is a struggle to make oneself understood and to understand the child. It is hearing the child scream, "I hate you," and feeling the inner echo which silently says, "I don't like you either right now." It is having one's routine upset. No more time to sip the morning coffee—it is gulped amid a clatter of, "My pants don't fit," and, "I need a quarter for the school party." Nor is there a quiet moment, upon returning from work, to read the mail or just sit and let the day's events sink in. Rather, it is a flurry of picking up the child, assessing her homework, beginning dinner, and seeing that the homework is done and her bath completed. By 8:00, lights are out in her room. Exhaustion...sitting in front of the TV... dozing. It is surprises—a little person climbing into bed with me. It is a plaintive, "Mommy, I'm sick," with the instant panic reverberating in me—I have to be a work at nine o'clock. Now what? Quick assessment. How sick? Can someone come in? Frantic phone calls—someone comes; I leave. The day is just beginning and I feel I've used up half my energy already. It is pride—"Yes, she is my daughter." Seeing her in the school play, full of eagerness. Seeing her walk in the choir procession on Sundays, eyes bright, head high. Knowing that only the night before there had been a tantrum, a wet bed, or an episode of stealing.

Gradually, there are moments of unexpected closeness. A hug which really carried love with it. Patting the brow, smoothing the forehead, holding a very little child in a rocking chair and singing her to sleep. The bonds begin to forge gradually out of looking at the sleeping child and thinking, "How beautiful she is." It is the consistency and constancy of relationship. If things go badly in the morning before school, there is the evening when things can go better. And, in any case, the child comes home because it is home, and I welcome her because this is where she belongs. It is moments of noting courage. She goes up to a friend's house and asks to play. She is turned away, and comes back to the car with some "doctored" story which says, "I'm not hurt, it's O.K." And I say, "Well, let's go home now." It is a child saying, "If they call me bad names, it doesn't hurt me," and squaring her tiny shoulders. It is turning to ask her to do something—working together. "O.K., I'll help you change your bed if you will start the breakfast." It is seeing her run, tassle on her cap, cheeks rosy and eyes shining, into the library to return some books, and running pell mell back to the car. It is seeing a comical little smile when someone says, "You two don't look at all alike," when looking at her and me. It is finally realizing that "I really love her. The miracle has happened—I really love her. She is my child."

2
Adoption: An Overview

For a child, adoption is an unparalleled opportunity to move from a life of neglect and poverty to a situation where parents want to nurture and the community has resources for helping the child develop. For parents who are unable to have children biologically, adoption is the ideal solution.

Many factors enter into the decision to adopt, and into the type of child a parent seeks. Thus, some parents seek and seem to need a handicapped child whom they can help, while other parents believe they could not cope with such a youngster. Adoption may be a way of expressing nonconformity, of fulfilling a social need, or simply of having the opportunity to be a parent. Probably most adopting parents have a mixture of motivations. It is generally accepted that the healthiest motivation is a desire to nurture and to parent. Many people believe that adopting an infant is easiest since this most closely parallels the experience of having a biological child, and that adopting an older child presents more difficulties for both child and parent in the adjustment process (Freud; Jewett).

Although providing a home and parenting to a child who is hard to place (e.g., an older child, a child of minority or mixed race, or a handicapped child) is obviously of great social usefulness, parents who take such a child may be more likely to encounter difficulties in many spheres of the bonding process. However, they also have a very special satisfaction when the child later begins to prosper. They can remember the beginnings, which may be the very stark experience of dealing with physical or emotional handicaps, or a combination of these.

Many obstacles stand in the way of adoption, the greatest being the recent marked decline in the number of adoptable normal healthy infants. The two main reasons for this are: 1) many children born out of wedlock are now brought up by their biological mothers (a situation which can be positive but which sometimes overburdens young women who are not ready for the responsibilities of parenthood and who therefore may neglect their children), and 2) birth control, which has greatly lessened the number of unwanted children in industrialized nations. The demand for normal white infants is especially strong, and many couples wait five years or longer for such a baby. At the same time, the number of older children and handicapped children available for adoption is increasing as more of them are viewed as adoptable, and as some young unmarried mothers, finding child care too difficult, finally place their offspring for adoption. In many agencies the average age of children awaiting adoption is 12. Children with severe handicaps like Down's syndrome and cerebral palsy are increasingly being adopted.

Agencies

"We waited three years for our baby. Then one day our agency called and told us to pick him up the next day. My husband had fallen and broken his leg, and it was in a cast. We went anyway. We didn't dare not to, after waiting so long. A neighbor lent us some baby things."

Adoption agencies are becoming increasingly selective about the people they will approve of as adoptive parents, demanding that they meet more stringent qualifications than formerly as to age, education, and socioeconomic resources. People wishing to adopt normal babies are aware that they are in a highly competitive situation since many other prospective parents are also seeking these children. One couple, highly advantaged educationally, socially, and economically, were advised that they would not be considered because the husband was 48. His wife was 38.

Agencies are the most important source of adoptable children, despite the fact that more and more children are adopted overseas or through private sources such as physicians and lawyers who are in touch with pregnant women who wish to place their babies for adoption.

Agencies' functions involve serving the best interests of the child, which means finding the best home available in the circumstances. What the agency believes will constitute the best home reflects current social values. Thus, a home headed by an older person, a single person, or a person from a racial minority may be viewed as inferior, even though a child may prosper in such a home.

What is it like to visit an agency? To hope for a child and to realize that those hopes may not be realized? Many prospective parents approach agencies with anxiety and a fear of rejection, for they have heard of others, in circumstances similar to their own, who did not succeed in adopting. The agency has power which would ordinarily reside with the individual. Parents who wish to conceive a child do not need to report their income or provide medical and perhaps psychological evidence of fitness. In an agency, a private family matter—the desire for a child—becomes a matter to discuss with strangers. Usually the prospective parents are asked to describe the type of child they want, and this initiates a discussion of the types of children available. The descriptions of available children are often quite discouraging, as one hears of mental retardation and various neurological disorders.

People who apply for a child become very vulnerable. They hope, yet try to suppress hope for fear of disappointment. The vagueness of the waiting period contributes to anxiety. A biological pregnancy takes nine months. Waiting to adopt might take several months or several years. Biological heritage places certain definable limits on expectations concerning the child: even though the child may be born with a handicap, it will certainly reflect his or her parents'

race and ethnicity. For adoptive parents, there are no such boundaries. They may request a child under one year old but be told that
the only child available for them is eight—actually, the child may turn
out to be ten. Any racial background is possible, and handicaps are
not uncommon. The prospective parents thus enter a situation of high
risk and great uncertainty, but also one of excitement and possibility.

The adoption agency is usually the setting for meeting the
child—an experience which parents describe as unforgettable. The
way the initial experience is handled can greatly affect the subsequent relationship of parents and child. Are staff supportive or indif-
ferent? Is there an effort to reassure, to help, or is the first meeting
handled with abruptness and haste? Is there an opportunity for significant persons in the family to be present?

Adoptions which are carried out in the United States require a
trial period, usually of one year, before the adoption can become legal
During this time, the child and the parents are under the supervision
of the adoption agency, whose recommendation is crucial in determining whether the parents may legally adopt the child. Because of
this, mothers may fear to discuss problems they may be having
with their child. The agency also has the role of counseling and advis-
ing the parents and generally facilitating the adoption. Thus, on one
hand, the agency functions as counselor and facilitator; on the other,
it provides recommendations to the court concerning whether the
adoption should become a legal and permanent bond. The power of
the agency, therefore, is very great in determining the final outcome.
(We will return to a discussion of the dual role of the agencies later,
in Chapter 5, as they greatly affect the adoptive experience.)

Foreign Adoptions

"We adopted in South America. We went down—fortunately,
my husband could come with me. We took a taxi to the agency,
where the baby was placed in my lap. We filled out some papers
and left. It was all very strange, almost an unreal experience. We
never saw anyone from the agency again; we came right home."

"We adopted overseas. Our baby was very sick when we got
there and we had to put him in a hospital right away. We hired

private nurses around the clock. We were over there, far from everyone we knew, dealing with a foreign language, an unfamiliar health care system, a new baby. But we came through it—we had to.''

Some prospective parents, realizing that their opportunities to adopt in the United States through agencies are slight or nonexistent, seek to adopt privately or in a foreign country. Often the children live in developing nations where material resources are minimal and where neglect and abuse are severe and common. Adoption is not possible for most of these children unless they are accepted by foreigners.

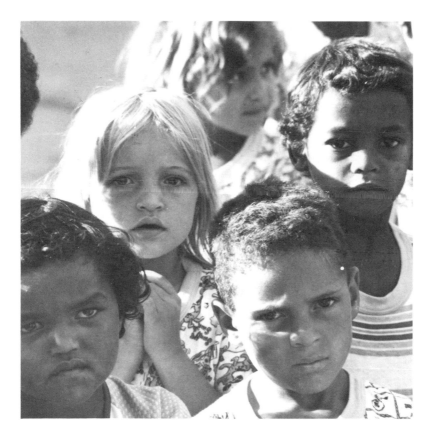

Foreign adoptions often present prospective parents with especially high risks because of the very complicated process of intercountry adoption and because the pre-adoptive assessment of the children's physical and psychological condition is often minimal. In addition, when a child finally becomes available, sometimes there is no waiting period and no agency supervision or agency help once the child is adopted. The child is adopted, legally, abroad, thus binding parents and child at the start of the relationship.

According to Margaret Ward, the experience of culture shock can be severe for the older child who is adopted from a foreign county. The child loses all familiar signs and symbols governing social interaction, thus adding greatly to his stress. When the child simultaneously loses contact with his native language, the transition is likely to be very difficult. Ward describes the sequence of culture shock as: 1) an initial phase of happiness and excitement when the child is interested in exploring his new surroundings but expects to return to the old environment; 2) a period of hostility and aggression as the child finds that his old ways do not fit the new situation and he is subjected to loss and frustration; and, 3) a gradual period of adaptation and resocialization. Ward points out that during this process both the child and the family change in a process of mutual accommodation.

Adopting a Handicapped Child

The handicapped child presents particular challenges. Until recently, children with major handicaps such as Down's syndrome and cerebral palsy were not considered for adoption and, if abandoned by their biological parents, were cared for in institutions or foster homes. Prospective parents of low priority (that is, older or single persons) may be virtually certain of being considered only for a handicapped child, although they will probably have a choice of the type of handicap they believe they are best able to cope with. Thus, ironically, the most difficult children tend to be placed in situations which have more than usual stresses and fewer than usual resources. While this paradox is widely acknowledged, the competitive nature of the adoptive situation in the United States makes it inevitable.

Saying that one can deal with a handicapped child is far different from experiencing the daily reality of doing so, and parents may find that the care of such a child, though rewarding, is also emotionally, physically, and financially taxing. Since the parents have voluntarily accepted the handicapped child, assistance and support may be less readily available from family and friends, whose comment may be, "Well, you asked for it, didn't you?" Because most adoptive parents are middle and upper middle class, they are ordinarily ineligible for any assistance with the costs of caring for a handicapped child, other than private insurance.

Since biological parenting is acknowledged to be one of life's most demanding and difficult tasks, how likely is it that there can be "absolutely no problems" in rearing a handicapped child? Yet adoptive parents, who perhaps do not feel as free as biological parents to discuss the problems they are experiencing, do sometimes make such statements, and even some of the literature available to prospective adoptive parents avoids discussing potential problems.

Adopting Transracially

Transracial adoptions, which in the late 1960s and early 1970s were helping to remove hard-to-place black and biracial children from public institutions to permanent families, all but disappeared by 1976, according to Simon and Altstein, who attribute this to organized efforts by black and Indian leaders to terminate such adoptions. Thus, the adoptions across racial lines that occurred in the '60s and '70s provide examples of atypical adoptive situations. Because of racial polarization, such adoptions are probably subject to additional social stress, which may complicate the adaptation of child and parents. Nevertheless, the study by Simon and Altstein points to some highly positive outcomes for both parents and children, not least of which is a diminution of racial prejudice among both the non-white children and their adoptive white parents.

Adopting an Older Child

Many problems face the child who is adopted after infancy, among them the need to compete with children who have had a more favorable start in life. Adopted children ordinarily come from environments of very limited opportunity, such as foster homes with as many as ten or twelve children, or institutions. The differences in lifestyles, values, and expectations between such environments and that of those seeking to adopt is often very wide and contributes not only to the joys but also to some problems of adoption when the adoptee is an older child.

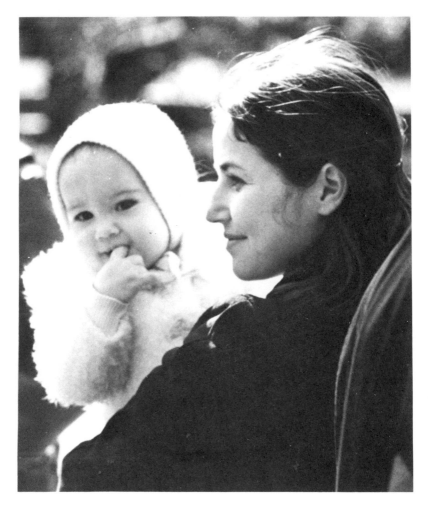

Our society is highly competitive, and from the moment a new child enters a school or a neighborhood there is a process of competing with other children. In school, adopted children may be singled out or different and as more likely to have problems. Children who come into a middle-class environment from poverty and neglect do so with serious deficits which cannot be made up quickly. They need a great deal of support and help. A child who knows that his biological parents placed him for adoption, or, as frequently happens, does not know who his biological parents are, is burdened by serious obstacles not faced by non-adopted children.

While the older child may experience an especially stressful time in the first years of adoption, the experience is within the child's memory and awareness. Contrary to popular stereotypes, an older, disadvantaged child may not show gratitude and happiness initially in the new environment, but with growing maturity, the child may come to have a deep appreciation of the opporutnities which adoption has provided. Such children may also develop a particularly caring and concerned attitude towards others, having known what it is like to be hungry and unloved. They may develop a greater understanding of the breadth of human experience than the average middle class child.

Social Issues Raised by Adoption

Undoubtedly, social attitudes play a major role in determining the success of adoption. Is the adoptive parent accorded the same recognition, respect, and consideration as a biological parent by school personnel? Do others in the community clearly recognize the child's place in the adoptive home and respect parental rights and decisions? Are neighbors easygoing and spontaneous in referring to "your mother" or "your father" when speaking to the child? Do others feel free to interfere in family matters, such as discipline, in ways they might not if the child were biologically related to the parents? If the child is in any way atypical in the community in terms of race or ethnic background, how readily can neighbors and the rest of the community accept this difference?

When a child is born there are many rituals and ceremonies to mark his entrance into the family—birth announcements, showers, religious rituals, etc. If the mother worked outside the home prior to delivery, she ordinarily has a period of time at home with her new baby; this is recognized as physiologically and psychologically necessary. What rituals surround the arrival of an adopted child, particularly an older child? Often there are none. The child arrives and gradually the process of becoming part of the family begins. The mother usually has no maternity leave, a factor of particular significance when the mother is the main or the sole source of financial support.

Families may, of course, evolve their own ceremonies to welcome the newly adopted child. Sometimes, however, parents who have waited for years to adopt will receive a call with instructions to pick up the child the next day. Frantic efforts to get a crib and some clothes together can add stress and hurry at a time when some leisure and stability are important.

What of the reactions of family members and friends? Do they take the role they would ordinarily take in welcoming a new baby in the family? Where there is prejudice against adopted children and their parents, it is perhaps a reflection of social attitudes toward out-of-wedlock births (since many adopted chidren are in this category), perhaps a reflection of, "Well, if his parents didn't keep him there must be something wrong with him," or perhaps a basic mistrust of any non-traditional family. Adoptive parents often note that, when their child is mentioned in the local press, he is ordinarily described as their adopted child. People who describe biological parents, but not adoptive parents, as "real" parents display a similar type of bias.

Does society have a stake in furthering and supporting adoption, or is it simply a private matter in which prospective parents and waiting children must cope as best they can? Because adoption offers the only way that homeless children can attain a real family life, it seems obvious that society does have a stake in its support. Programs such as subsidized adoption for especially hard-to-place children, like those with severe handicaps, are beginning to develop. What of worldwide coordination for adoption? Does it really make sense to deny the needs of children when there are adults who are eager to meet their needs but who happen to live in another county? Is it possible to have more international planning to facilitate the adoption of children in need? Currently, only the most stalwart and persistent prospective parents, and those who can afford the costs, can under-take the adoption of a foreign child. The paperwork required by each government is prodigious. Are there ways to circumvent some of the tedious and costly and difficult aspects of adopting overseas? Greater societal support for adoption could result in a quite different empha-sis from the present one where children are shunted from one foster home to another, and where prospective parents are told "there are no children" while thousands of children over the world die of hunger. Since we simply do not have enough adoptive agencies, especially in underdeveloped nations, to deal with the children in need, it is only the lucky few who are actually adopted.

The decision to adopt a disadvantaged child affects the com-munity, since children with problems absorb a disproportionate share of the time of teachers and school counselors. A child who arrives with no knowledge of English will require additional help until he or she becomes proficient in the language. Communities differ in their willingness to meet these needs, especially if the child is handicapped or ethnically different from the majority of residents.

Children Who Are Not Adopted

What may become of the children who are not adopted? In a study of 624 children who entered foster care and who were followed for five years, Frank found that 80 percent were seriously psychologically disturbed and that almost all of them deteriorated psychologically over the five-year period. Treatment (such as counseling) available to these children was judged to be very inadequate. At the time of the study (1979), over $9,000 in public funds was being spent yearly to care for each child. Bush points out that children who are sent to long-term institutions for treatment of emotional disturbances tend to deteriorate rather than to improve. It seems likely that children who are in situations where resources for their care are strained may be especially vulnerable to abuse. Kinard points out that abused chil-dren have a significantly lower self-concept than non-abused chil-dren. Thus adoption offers opportunities to children which are not likely to be found in foster care and institutions, and presents more favorable conditions for the growth and development of the child.

3

Some Theories about Bonding

Although the theories discussed in this chapter relate primarily to the attachment between biological mothers and their infants, many aspects of these theories are relevant to bonding with an adopted child.

In 1976, Marshall Klaus and John Kennell published *Maternal-Infant Bonding*, a book that ushered in a new era of maternity care. Parents and professionals alike embraced the authors' concept that early togetherness of the family unit "attaches" (bonds) the infant to mother, father, and siblings. Studies done by a variety of investigators verified that separating parents from their newborn infant had negative effects on future parenting activities and child development.

Today, many hospital maternity units manifest an understanding of bonding by allowing immediate maternal-infant contact in the delivery room, father presence in the delivery room, frequent in-hospital visits by the father and siblings, and increased opportunities for the father to room-in on the traditional maternity unit. Bonding theories have also contributed to the development of innovative types of maternity care, such as birthing centers or in-hospital birthing rooms where particular emphasis is given to a homelike environment that includes the presence and participation of the father and siblings.

In *Maternal-Infant Bonding*, Klaus and Kennell began to identify the factors that might contribute to a poor bonding experience between mothers and their infants. These include mother-infant separation immediately after birth due to illness of the mother or the baby, unresolved grief in the mother, and obstacles to attachment engendered by caretakers or hospital regulations. However, many questions remain unanswered. Primary among them is, how do individuals who are not present at a child's birth bond to that child? This is an important question for adoptive parents who are, of course, separated from their adopted children for some period of time after birth. Are all adoptive parents at risk for future parenting problems because they missed being with the child immediately after birth? Or is there a sensitive period in the adoptive experience when a similar attachment process can occur? Are some adoptive children/parents more at risk for bonding than others, and, if so, what differentiates a high-risk bonding situation from a low-risk one? Finally, is the process of bonding with biological parents different in any way from the process of bonding with adoptive parents? Answers to such questions are important to adoptive parents and health care professionals working with both biological and adoptive parents.

Theories about the nature of the bonding process and the factors that might affect it include hypotheses about: 1)the process of bonding; 2) how children are affected by early maternal deprivation; 3) the effects of fetal-maternal interactions on future bonding and attachment; 4) how the mother's personality structure and her motivation for having children affect bond formation; and 5) the effects of environmental factors on bonding.

The Process of Bonding

What is the actual process of bonding and how does it relate to the adoption situation? Klaus and Kennell (1976) identified behaviors related to bonding which occur at four specific time periods before and after a baby's birth: Time 1, Prior to Pregnancy; Time 2, Pregnancy; Time 3, Birth; and Time 4, After Birth. These period can be generalized into the following time sequences in the adoptive situation: Time 1, Prior to Entry; Time 2, Entry; and Time 3, After Entry.

Time 1, Prior to Entry (Pre-adoption)

At this phase, most behaviors of both the biological and adoptive mothers may be identical. An adoptive mother will need to assume the role of mother just as a biological mother does, and her concepts of mothering, her feminine identity, her experience with children, and her relation with her own mother will all be relevant factors in attaining the maternal role.

Positive fantasizing by biological mothers about the child-to-be is seen as important in developing a bond with their infants. Is fantasy as possible and as useful for adoptive mothers? Biological mothers problem-solve through fantasy production. Do adoptive mothers also do the "work of worry" through fantasizing about realistic problems they may experience with an adopted child (that is, problems about language barriers, health, and other matters)? Uncertainty about the status of adoption and the child-to-be may make fantasizing difficult, which may interfere with future nurturing behaviors. How does the adoptive mother prepare for the child-to-be?

Support groups, which are important before a child is born as well as after, are seen as another essential in aiding mother-infant bonding in the biological parenting situation. What support groups are important in the pre-adoptive situation?

Time 2, At Entry (Adoption)

At the birth of an infant, many activities can occur which will foster attachment between parents and infant. What is the entry period like for adoptive parents and children, and what may the effects be on bonding? One factor would be the mother's role in the first meeting with the child—is she active and in control of the situation, or is she helpless and confused? Another factor will be the supporting persons present at the first meeting of mother and child and their reactions to the child. The adoptive father's acceptance or rejection of the child will be especially important to the mother at this time. Further, what support does she get from professionals, especially the agency social worker, during and immediately following this first encounter, and what caretaking activities can she begin? All these factors enter into the attachment process in the biological entry period, and may be operant, either positively or negatively, in the adoptive entry period.

Time 3, After Entry (After Adoption)

In this period, we can again gain some clues from biological bonding which may foster bonding of adoptive mothers and children. In essence, to facilitate attachment, the mother communicates with the child both verbally and non-verbally, touches or nurtures the child in some fashion, identifies the child as belonging to the family, and works out a harmonious routine of interaction with the child. In the adoptive situation, such factors are also present, but are subject to wide variations. How do these variations affect the bond formed between parent and child?

The Three Stages of Bonding in Adoption

Time 1.   Bonding Activities Prior to Adoption

1. Mother attains role identity
2. Mother fantasizes about infant/child-to-be
3. Mother problem-solves through fantasy
4. Mother problem-solves through manipulating environment
5. Mother develops a support group
6. Mother carries out nesting behaviors (prepares infant's/child's clothes, room, etc.)

Time 2.   Bonding Activities at Entry (Adoption)

1. Mother is active participant and maintains control
2. Mother has opportunity for immediate and prolonged contact with infant/child
3. Significant others are present
4. Significant others acknowledge/give attention to infant/child

 5. Significant others acknowledge/give attention to mother
 6. Mother begins to nurture
 7. Father interacts and begins to nurture infant/child
 8. Attendant professionals give support

Time 3. Bonding Activities after Adoption

A. Mother

 1. Touches and explores infant/child
 2. Engages in non-verbal communication
 3. Engages in verbal communication (high-pitched voice for infant)
 4. Allows body contact with infant/child
 5. Interacts in rhythmic patterns with infant
 6. "Identifies" infant/child
 7. Feeds, bathes, clothes infant/child

B. Infant/Child

 1. Engages in non-verbal or verbal communication with mother
 2. Responds to maternal nurturing behaviors
 3. Elicits physiological response in mother
 4. Infant meets mother's rhythms

The child also communicates—nonverbally in all cases and verbally in the case of an older child—by responding in some manner to mothering activities, by eliciting responses from the mother, and by working out a routine for interaction with the family unit. Perhaps variations of these behaviors in the adoptive situation is even greater for children than for mothers. The manner in which a child responds or fails to respond is determined by many complex factors—the child's age, previous experience and development, and innate characteristics. The variations in these behaviors may foster or impede bonding. It will be important to identify the behaviors of the child that help and those that hinder attachment in the adoptive situation.

Klaus' principles of monotropy (the tendency to attach to one child at a time) and time-giving may also affect the progress of bonding between adoptive mothers and children. Does the mother have to attach to more than one child at a time? Is she grieving a loss while attempting to bond with the new child? Does her schedule permit her to spend time with her child? What is the quality of the interaction regardless of the time spent?

In summary, the bonding process between adopted parents and children is hypothesized to contain components similar to those in the bonding process between biological parents and children. Variations are expected in the adoptive situation—some fostering bonding, some blocking bonding. Analysis of our research will shed some light on these questions and help adoptive parents and the professionals who work with them understand and facilitate bonding with an adopted child.

The Effects of Early Maternal Deprivation

One of the first to study the attachment process was John Bowlby. In contrast to Klaus and Kennell, Bowlby (1966) looked at the process in terms of how the child attaches itself to the parent, primarily to the mother. Through clinical and other studies, Bowlby and his associates studied how separating the child from its parents affects the child's mental health. They concluded that these effects could indeed be severe, and identified the times in children's lives when they were most likely to be deeply harmed by maternal deprivation. They stated that the second half of the first year of life is the age at which an infant will sustain the most severe damage to its mental and physical development if it is deprived of mothering by one significant individual. By contrast, a school-age child who is separated from his mother for some days or months, as during hospitalization, may be negatively affected for overall personality development, but in a less severe and permanent manner. Thus, according to Bowlby, the age of the child and the length of the separation will determine the degree of risk to the future development of the child.

Bowlby describes the child who has been deprived of mothering for a prolonged period of time at an early age as having no real feeling for others and no capacity to care for people or to make true friends; as maintaining an inaccessibility which exasperates those trying to help; as having no emotional response to situations where such a response would be normal; as having a curious lack of concern for others; as being deceitful and evasive; of stealing without apparent reason; and of lack of concentration at school. According to Bowlby, if a child does not form an attachment to a parent or parent substitute within a specific time period, he/she will be forever handicapped in forming relationships. Bowlby and others, such as Spitz and Wolf, supply a complementary theory to the bonding process described by Klaus and Kennell. Not only does the nurturer (mother) have a sensitive period in which to attach herself to an infant or child, but the infant or child also has a sensitive period to attach itself to a nurturer. The relationship is reciprocal—a two-way process. If attachment fails to occur in either individual—nurturer or child—the relationship is in jeopardy. Even more important for the child, Bowlby said, all future relations will be in jeopardy, since inability to attach becomes a life-long pattern.

Bowlby's material presents a very bleak picture for the child separated from a nurturing parent. However, many theorists do not subscribe to his views, and, in fact, find many shortcomings in his work. M.D. Ainsworth identified some major problems inherent in Bowlby's theory. First, says Ainsworth, Bowlby seems to imply that all children who are separated from a parent or mother are deprived. This, however, is far from reality, especially if we see deprivation, as Ainsworth does, as "relationships or interactions of insufficient quality and quantity" (p. 291). A child can be separated from a "permanent" parent and not be deprived of meaningful relationships if the environmental circumstances are favorable, or if a stable nurturer is present or if the child's personality is particularly resilient. For example, a child in a warm, loving foster home, even though the home is not permanent, may experience few of the effects of deprivation. Further, children in institutions which supply meaningful stimulation and stable, involved caretakers or nurses, may also suffer few ill effects. Finally, some children, because of innate characteristics, previous experiences, and personality development, will be resilient to the effects of deprivation. On the other hand, children who are with a permanent mother without separations may still be deprived if the quality of the relationship is poor. Continuity of a parent's presence does not insure the quality of the relationship.

Problematic also is Bowlby's theory of the degrees of damage to future development caused by maternal deprivation. Research cited by Ainsworth indicates that the assumption that deprivation affects all processes of development equally is unjustified since any degree of damage which occurs is affected by many factors: the child's disposition and strengths; the differences in the child's environment before and after deprivation occurs; and the child's previous pattern of development. Under favorable circumstances, one may expect a minimum degree of damage from being deprived of maternal care.

Finally, while Bowlby apparently believes that personality patterns emerging from deprivation are irreversible, research and theory from many fields seem to indicate that the opposite actually seems to be the case in that many problems emerging from early separation experiences are, indeed, reversible when relief from the deprivation is provided (Fischer, 1952; Tremitiere, 1979). Further, many problems that evolve from deprivation may never really be seen in the child's behavior, and, in fact, may only emerge in unusual life situations. Ainsworth states:

A deprivation experience acts through its influence upon ongoing processes and is interpreted in the light of previous experience. The ongoing processes upon which it acts are, in turn, a result of the whole previous history of development that has taken place through the interaction of the organism (and its genetically determined structure) with environmental influences. The response to relief from deprivation is determined both by the processes set up in the course of the deprivation experience and by the extent to which they are reinforced, modified or reversed by later organism-environment interaction. All of these influences are important in determining the eventual outcome.

M. Rutter supports Ainsworth's conclusions, and believes that the reversibility of the effects of deprivation is related to such factors as the child's emotions and thinking processes, the level of stimulation and support in the environment, and the age of the child when deprivation occurs. Although reversal becomes less likely the longer deprivation lasts and the older the child is when removed from the situation, varying degrees of reversal may still occasionally occur in older children.

In writing about adoption and the older child, C.L. Jewett indicates that the effects of privation may be reversible. According to Jewett, one way to accomplish this is to see that the child is carefully and harmoniously matched with the adoptive parents, so that a good reciprocal relationship between parent and child will develop. If the parent and child are in synchrony with each other, the relation will flow more easily, and the effects of deprivation may be alleviated more quickly.

Margaret Mead, the well-known cultural anthropologist, gives an interesting perspective on how lacking one permanent or stable mother may affect a child's development. Mead feels, based on her cross-cultural studies, that there may be some advantage to diffusion of child care. She suggests that, in contrast to the view that an exclusive mother-child relation within a nuclear family is the only satisfactory method of raising a child, group methods of child rearing and multiple mother figures may actually ensure the child of greater continuity of care with less likelihood of trauma. Instead of all the burden of mothering being on one individual, the burden is shared among several nurturers. What a child misses from one nurturer, he may get from another. Also, multiple mother figures, according to Mead, may produce a child capable of establishing more flexible relationships with a wider variety of individuals. She is, of course, speaking of stable cultural groups, where the group assumes responsibility for child care.

Several individuals who have investigated group care of children in other countries support some of Mead's views. M. Wolins looked at five different types of group care settings for children in Austria, Israel, Poland, and Yugoslavia. His findings indicate that, in general, children in these group care settings (who had no "permanent" mother or caretaker in the traditional sense) showed no intellectual or psychosocial differences when compared with children reared by one mother in a nuclear home environment. In fact, in some cases, group-reared children measured higher than did home-reared children on certain variables of intellectual development, personality development, and value development.

It seems, then, that there is a great diversity of opinion as to whether separation (deprivation) of a child from a permanent mother figure for certain periods of the child's life causes negative effects. When negative effects do occur, as they usually do in situations where a child must be placed for adoption, questions remain concerning their reversibility, the factors which contribute to or mitigate their effects, and which individuals will be most vulnerable to undesirable effects. The picture, however, is much less dismal than the one originally painted by Bowlby, and it seems possible that the effects of deprivation can be partially or completely overcome in many, if not all, situations. Thus, there remains great hope that the adopted child, in spite of separations suffered in the past, may develop the capacity for bonding to the adopted parent, and for evolving normal interpersonal relationships.

The Effects of Fetal-Maternal Interaction on Bonding

Another set of theories is important to this investigation. Klaus and Kennell and others believe that pregnancy is the point where mother-infant bonding begins—that is, the mother and her fetus are hypothesized to have a relationship prenatally that will affect the attachment process after the infant is born. Benedek (1970) and others have described the maternal-fetal unit as a psychobiological one, implying that physiology plays an important role in the evolving relationship. A study by Fawcett indicates that fathers-to-be may undergo psychological changes similar to those of mothers-to-be, obviously without actually carrying the fetus. Some investigators (Rubins, Caplan,

Benedek) have pointed to the role of fantasy in influencing the fetal-parental relations, demonstrating that the manner in which a mother fantasizes about her infant-to-be may have positive or negative implications for the relationship she develops with her infant after its birth. Fantasizing realistically and positively about caring for and nurturing the infant seems to aid the attachment or bonding process while suppressing fantasies or having unrealistically positive or negative fantasies seems to be a block to bonding.Thus, fantasizing about the infant-to-be seems to be an important mechanism in beginning the future relationship between parent and child. Further, it does not seem to be totally dependent upon an actual physiological link with a fetus within the body.

The Effects of the Mother's Personality Structure on Bonding

In another body of literature, theoreticians indicate that the personality structures of parents and their motivations for having children can have an effect on the process of attaching or bonding to the infant. Many authors (Lipkin, MacFarlane, Mahler) have identified both good and poor motivations for parenthood. A readiness to give of oneself to develop the next generation is seen by Eric Erikson (1968) as the adult task of "generativity"—a highly evolved and necessary function. In addition, the desire to nurture and to fulfill biological, social and/or cultural roles are also cited as good motivations for parenthood. Other motivations for attainment of parenthood include fear of voluntary or involuntary infertility, a desire to make up for a lack of meaningful marital partnership, a wish to have proof of being "really a man/woman," and a wish for the status ascribed to the parental role.

The personalities of adoptive parents also affect the process of bonding. Thus, the emotional and intellectual maturity of the parents (Erikson, 1963; Bowlby, 1966), their degree of ego strength, and the degree to which they have matured and developed individual identities separate from *their* parents (Schecter) will affect their motivation and readiness for parenthood (Bowlby, 1966) and will affect the evolving parent-child relationship and the attachment that may occur.

The Effects of Environmental Factors on Bonding

The final area of theory which may shed light on factors affecting bonding between parent and child deals with the effect of environmental factors on the parent-child relationship, particularly the presence or absence of support systems and environmental stressors. According to one investigator, the process of becoming parents, which was once a transition period carefully worked out with traditions of support from the extended family, is now in a crisis, with few societal mechanisms for helping parents cope with the profound changes and developmental conflicts (Bibring). Isolated nuclear families in the United States may not have anyone at all with whom they can talk about their problems. To alleviate this sad state of affairs, a number of organizations have sprung up which, concerning themselves with the process of pregnancy and parenthood, have partially replaced the extended family in supporting prospective parents. Bonds between couples made in these organizations often continue for years (Klaus and Kennell, 1976).

Family stress of any kind—moving to a new area, marital infidelity, financial worries, death—may delay bond formation with an infant or child at the crucial time when he or she is introduced into the family unit (Cohen).

In addition, one must consider the effects of a new environment on an older child's ability to bond. If the child has been adopted from a foreign country, he/she will be experiencing culture shock from the totally different and alien environment, a shock intensified by an inability to communicate in his/her native language. Even if the child is not from a foreign country, the new environment is likely to be different from the old one. For example, to a child from an impoverished environment, having a private bedroom, toys, and enough to eat may be a sensory overload. The stress of so many new stimuli, even though they are positive and given with the best intentions, may prove to be more than the child can cope with.

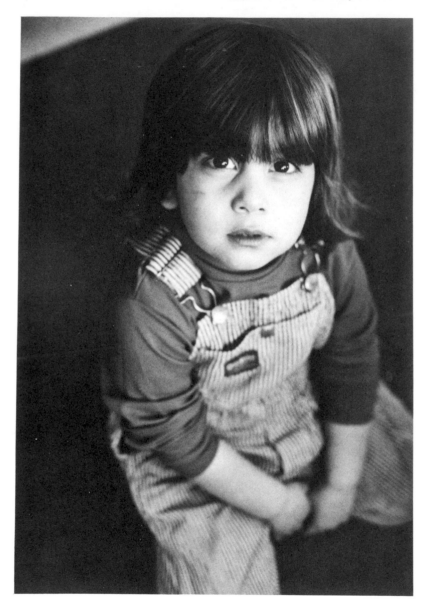

4

Conducting the Study

According to the theories discussed in Chapter 3, many factors affect the bonding process. In the mother, these include psychosexual development, personality, motivation for becoming a parent, and preparation for the maternal role, including fantasizing about the child. In the child, they include life history, background, culture, and past attachments. In addition, interactions between mother and child influence the bonding process. These interactions are greatly affected by support systems or lack of them, and by environmental stressors, such as change, loss, or conflict. The common behaviors which help bonding in biological situations provide a framework for observing similar or different behaviors in the adoptive situation in the three time periods of relating with a child—Time 1, Prior to Entry; Time 2, At Entry, and Time 3, After Entry.

Based on the above, the following study questions guided our inquiry:

1. How does bonding differ, if at all, in biological and adoptive bonding?

2. Are there differences in bonding with a young child/infant as compared with an older child?
3. What factors facilitate or block bonding between adoptive mothers and children?

Purpose and Participation

Our study was designed to obtain information from adoptive mothers about the process of bonding, or attaching, to their children. Since we were interested in tapping data from as many people as possible, minimal sampling restrictions were employed. Our only requirement for participation was that the mother had had her child for at least one year.

To solicit volunteers for the study, we appealed to a variety of adoptive parents' organizations for assistance. Some of the organizations publicized our project and called for volunteers in their newsletters or at their meetings. When possible, we personally attended these meetings to explain our study and request volunteers. Although we originally planned to conduct the survey in only one way—through taped interviews in the homes of volunteer participants—we soon began to receive requests to participate from adoptive mothers across the country. Not wishing to lose data from these sources, we sent out mail questionnaires, similar to our in-person interview format, to allow those mothers whom we could not personally interview to participate.

Later, we also sent out questionnaires to a small group of adopted children. The data obtained from the children is discussed in Chapter 6.

Sample

Requesting volunteer participation was the only ethical manner in which we could have conducted the study. However, using volunteers does introduce a certain amount of bias into the study. For instance, we must assume that our participants were not entirely representative of the entire population of adoptive mothers in the United States since volunteers are likely to be more open and more willing to discuss their feelings and perceptions than the average person. This being so, their ideas and perceptions about adoptive bonding might also be somewhat different from those of the average adoptive mother. Thus, the reader must use caution when making generalizations to him/herself and to other adoptive parents. Also, while we believe that many of our findings apply to bonding between fathers and adopted children, our sample included only mothers and therefore care must be taken in making generalizations to fathers. In addition, our mothers were different from the general population in that they were all white. Presently, increasing numbers of non-white families are adopting children. While it is highly probable that our findings have relevance for non-white mothers, the reader is again cautioned about generalizing.

There appeared to be some differences in economic status between our taped interviewees and our mail questionnaire respondents. Since we interviewed the mothers in their homes, the signs of material affluence made it quite evident that they were upper-middle class. Our questionnaire sample, however, gave many indications that this was not always the case with them. Such comments as, "The child helps on our farm," and, "We have ten children and live very simply," were clues that the questionnaire group had a more varied economic status. In addition, the questionnaire sample indicated that they had adopted more ethnically diverse, handicapped, and older children than had the interview sample.

Instrument Development and Forms

The interview items were developed from our review of the literature cited in Chapter 3, and thus demonstrate face validity. In addition, interaction with the adoptive parents allowed for refinement of items. Finally, some items evolved from current media coverage of adoption. A question dealing with the potential effects of open records, whereby an adopted child may legally seek to find his biological parents, is an example of this type of item. (See Appendix.)

Procedure for the Taped Interviews

Mothers who were interested in being interviewed were requested to give us their addresses and telephone numbers. We then contacted them by phone and further explained the project, the requirements for participation, parental rights, maintenance of anonymity, the interview format (including taping), and mentioned that we would need to have them sign a permission form. An appointment was arranged for an interview in the mother's home. Once there, we summarized the information discussed during the telephone conversation and obtained formal written permission to conduct and tape an interview. The interviews lasted approximately one hour, although some extended to one and a half or two hours. They were conducted in an informal, relaxed fashion so as to encourage the mothers to be as open as possible. We were able to facilitate the interview process by picking up and following leads and clues, both verbal and nonverbal, that we detected in the mothers' responses. In addition, we often met the adopted children, which gave us an opportunity to observe mother-child interactions and to obtain a "flavor" of the situation.

In some instances, however, our presence seemed to interfere with data collection. We found this to be the case when discussing open records with our interview sample. None of the mothers interviewed expressed a totally negative stance on the issue, which was not the case with mothers responding to the mail questionnaire. It is quite possible that our presence inhibited some mothers from expressing their true feelings and influenced them to respond in ways they assumed to be "socially desirable."

While it was not our intent to counsel those mothers who were troubled, in some instances we did function as supports during the interview and, if asked, suggested referral sources.

Procedure for Mail Questionnaire

Data collection with the questionnaire sample was somewhat less complex. In addition to those who wrote asking to participate, we obtained lists of volunteers' names, addresses, and telephone numbers from agencies and organizations. Individuals on the lists who indicated a willingness to participate in the study were mailed a letter containing an explanation of the study, a consent form, the question- naire, and a stamped envelope addressed to us. Respondents were assured of anonymity. Although not all mothers who were sent forms chose to return them, our response rate—92 percent—was excellent.

In some instances we followed up questionnaire returns with telephone contacts. This supplied us with additional insight on some responses.

One of our major sources of information, in both the interview and questionnaire sample groups, was our use of open-ended ques- tions, that is, questions that allowed the mothers to respond subjec- tively and at length. These questions supplied us with information indicating what the mothers (not the investigators) perceived as the important issues related to adoption and to developing a bond to a child. (See Appendix.)

Analysis of Data

Since this study was intended to be a very basic, exploratory study designed to provide facts in a area where little was previously known, no statistical analysis other than percentages was done on the data collected. The information gained from questioning mothers was treated as "nominal data," which means that we simply described it, put it into categories, and looked for patterns in the data.

The raw data obtained from both the mail questionnaires and the transcribed tapes of the interviews were sorted into the following categories.

Age of child now; sex of child
Length of time since adoption
Age at adoption
Race / ethnicity
Source of adoption (i.e., agency, private, etc.)
Handicaps
Fantasies about the child-to-come
First encounter experiences
Closeness factors

Distance factors
Attitudes towards adoption
Attitude towards open records
Support systems
Agency relationships
Suggestions for agencies
Other comments

We were then able to identify certain emerging patterns of responses in the various categories we had defined for the study. These patterns will be described and discussed in detail in the following chapter.

Of all the answers received, the most difficult to reduce to categories were those to the open-ended questions. These answers did yield, however, much rich and varied data, as will be seen in the next chapter.

5
The Study's Findings

In reviewing our study's findings, we will discuss items from the interviews and questionnaires according to the time period involved, that is Time 1, Prior to Entry; Time 2, At Entry; and Time 3, After Entry of the adopted child, and we will consider how the findings relate to the theoretical models of bonding discussed in Chapter 3.

Description of Sample

Our sample of mothers and children presented the following picture:

Table 5-1. Number of Mothers and Children Involved in the Study

	Interview Group	Questionnaire Group	Total
Mothers	60	57	117
Children	87	106	193

By sex, the children were divided as follows:

Table 5-2.   Sex of Children

	Interview Group	Questionnaire Group	Total
Male	42	39	81
Female	45	67	112
Total	87	106	193

Thus, the one hundred and seventeen mothers had adopted one hundred and ninety-three children, eighty-one of them male and one hundred and twelve of them female. The race and ethnicity of the children are shown in Table 5-3.

Table 5-3.   Race/Ethnicity of Children

	Interview Group	Questionnaire Group	Total
White	40	36	76
Oriental	15	28	43
Hispanic	22	12	34
Black/White mixed	9	25	34
Indian (North American)	0	4	4
Black	1	1	2
	87	106	193

The largest percentage of our study children (including three Canadians) were reported as white (39%). The interview group had a 12 percent lead in the number of white children adopted. The next largest ethnic category of children were Orientals (22%), including children from Korea, Thailand, Vietnam, and other Eastern countries. Here the questionnaire mothers had the lead, having adopted more Oriental children than interview mothers.

The other two large racial/ethnic groups adopted were black/white mixed and Hispanic children. In the black/white mixed group, the questionnaire mothers adopted at a 24 percent rate while the interview mothers adopted at a 10 percent rate. The situation was exactly reversed for Hispanic children, where interview mothers had adopted nearly twice as many such children as the questionnaire mothers. (Hispanic children included those from South and Central America as well as from Puerto Rico.)

Only one mother in each group reported that her adopted child was black. All four of the North American Indian children were adopted by mothers in the questionnaire group.

Combining the children adopted by both groups, the ages at adoption were:

Table 5-4.   Age at Adoption

	Number	Percent
Infant under 2 years	113	59%
2-5 years	33	17%
6-9 years	29	15%
10-13 years	18	9%
Total	193	100%

Age at adoption was a very important variable in our study, as it was related to various factors affecting attachment. We noted that only 59 percent had been adopted under the age of two—the "desirable" age many parents want. No one in the sample had adopted a child over thirteen years of age.

At the time of our study, the children had been adopted for the lengths of time indicated in Table 5-5 (again combining both groups).

Table 5-5.   Length of Time Since Adoption

	Number	Percent
Less than 2 years	60	31%
Between 2-5 years	94	49%
Between 6-9 years	25	13%
Between 10-13 years	14	7%
Total	193	100%

Handicaps

Of the total sample of children, one hundred and thirty-six (70%) were reported to have no handicaps. For the remaining fifty-seven, handicaps can be placed into emotional, physical, and intellectual disability categories. Several children were reported to have more than one handicap; for example, both a physical and an intellectual disability.

The total number of reported emotional handicaps was thirty-one (16%) (all of these children were adopted over age four). Some of these children were receiving or had received psychotherapy. Some examples of the reported difficulties were: extreme insecurity, bed wetting, school problems, rages, destructiveness, running away, stealing, or telling lies.

Thirty-two (about 17%) of the children were reported to have physical handicaps or disabilities. In many cases, the parents had been unaware of the handicap at the time of the adoption. The child was either handicapped when received, especially in foreign adoptions, or the disability turned up on a later examination. Some of the defects were correctable by medical attention, diet, or surgery. The conditions affecting these children included cerebral palsy, missing extremities, rickets, muscular dystrophy, heart defects, partial deafness, neurological impairment, strabismus, congenital hip dislocation, club foot, anemia, severe intractable diarrhea, hyperactivity and Down's syndrome. Nine children were reported to have intellectual disabilities. Four of these children had low IQs and five had learning disabilities.

Time 1: Prior to Entry

As discussed in Chapter 3, several important behaviors or events occur during Time 1, before the child enters the family but after he is expected, which may affect the process of bonding. While our questionnaire and interviews did not ask what the mothers' characteristics (such as role attainment or personality characteristics) were at this time, we did investigate the mothers' activities in preparing for the child. Fantasizing about the child-to-be is a primary form of preparation for any child, since it allows the prospective mother to work through possible problems and relations she might have with the new child, and may help her to find alternative solutions to issues which might arise in real life situations. Such fantasies literally allow for a "dress rehearsal" for when the child arrives. In addition, an image of the fantasy child allows for "nesting" behaviors, another form of preparation for the child. Nesting behaviors include buying equipment, bedding, clothes, toys, and other necessities. Questioning the adoptive mother about her fantasies about the child-to-be often brought up nesting behaviors as well as fantasies.

Fantasies

When asked about their fantasies before the arrival of the child, fifty (43%) mothers did not report any. Twenty-one of these mothers gave no reason, while the other twenty-nine indicated that they had actively suppressed fantasy production, usually for one of two reasons: 1) there was not enough time between being notified that the child was available and the child's arrival, and 2) they were afraid that the adoption would "fall through."

In the biological situation, repression of fantasy about the infant-to-be can signal a potentially problematic mother-infant relationship and provide a clue to a potential bonding risk. Do current adoption practices enhance such risks when they make it difficult for adoptive parents to fantasize about their child-to-be and engage in nesting behaviors? How can an adoptive parent fantasize about a child if she has one day's notice of the child's arrival, or if the parent fears that arrangements will fall through? How can parents prepare for a child whose attributes—size, sex, race, etc.—they cannot imagine? Since pre-entry attachment to the infant-to-be is important to biological parents in the overall process of establishing a relationship, it should make the process simpler for the adoptive parent (and child) as well.

Of mothers reporting fantasies, fifty-seven had fantasies that were realistic and positively-toned, for example: "I fantasized about what he'd look like; I was told he was cinnamon colored—I wondered what that meant." Some mothers' comments after meeting their children were: "He's beautiful;" "I imagined doing things together as a family;" "I fantasized holding him and feeding him."

Although very few mothers reported unrealistic fantasies ("I had some unrealistic fantasies; I was a teacher, so I thought I could solve all my child's problems easily"), there was often a discrepancy between the fantasized child and the child in reality: "He had strabismus. We didn't know this before we saw him. They brought him to us in a wheelchair. We were upset." Discrepancies between the "ideal" fantasized child and the "real" child take on special meaning in adoptive situations where the mother is not aware of her child's handicap when the child is adopted. In our sample, eleven mothers reported that the agency had misrepresented their child to them before the child entered the family. Such actions foster the gap between the ideal fantasy child and the real child, and may produce a block to bonding.

In summary, fantasy production in both biological and adoptive situations, when positively toned and realistic, may assist with pre-entry attachment to a child and with preparatory activiteis. Unrealistic fantasies, especially when there is a great gap between the ideal fantasy child and the real child, may make bonding more difficult.

Support Systems

Another factor which helps prepare a mother for the advent of a child is her support systems. A pregnant woman develops many support systems among family, friends, coworkers, health professionals, and others. Supporting others "initiate" the coming of a child for the mother-to-be with such rituals as the baby shower. Childbirth preparation classes may take the place of or supplement extended family groups for the expecting couple and provide much support for prospective parents throughout the childbirth experience.

The same situation is usually not true for the adoptive parent, however. Because those seeking to adopt are aware of the possibility that any one adoption might not be actualized, they often prefer to keep the possibility secret until they actually have the child. Thus, traditional support systems, such as family and friends, may not even be aware that the parents are seeking a child. In addition, there is no routine "maternity leave" for adoptive mothers and "child showers" and even baby showers are not common. Relatives and friends are often ambivalent about the adoption, and sometimes fail to provide help that most biological mothers routinely receive. While adoptive parents' groups may provide support, some groups are more like "information sorting" centers than groups designed to meet the emotional needs of prospective parents.

Since most adoptive mothers discussed support as it related to their situation *after* the child arrived, this information will be discussed in the section on "After Entry." It is important to remember, however, that support systems have a pervasive effect on the process of attaching to an adopted child. This factor will affect the process of bonding at all time phases—Before Entry, At Entry, and After Entry. The presence or absence of supports for the mother will make a difference in how easily she can bond with her adopted child.

Time 2: At Entry

The mothers' responses to our questions about their first encounter with their adopted children gave us some insight into the factors that affect eventual attachment. In the biological situation, it will be remembered, several factors affect the mother's ability to attach with her infant. Key among these are the ability of the mother to feel that she is active and in control of the situation, her ability to begin to nurture her infant immediately after the birth, and the presence of others who provide her with support and "emotional fuel."

First Encounter Experiences

An adoptive mother's descriptions of her first encounter with her child may give clues to their future relationship. Most mothers commented in some way on the appearance of their children as part of this first impression. "She looked so much like our family—coloring, hair, everything—that she really fit in." "When we first saw her she was screaming and her face was bright red. I felt some doubt, but my husband immediately accepted her, so I felt OK.'' "At first I was disappointed. My feeling was, 'Oh, no, this can't be my child.' She was very unattractive and she had been sick on the plane." "He was the most beautiful baby I had ever seen."

One is reminded again of the discrepancy between the ideal fantasy child and the real child. While adoptive mothers may be realistic about a child's general appearance relative to age, size, sex, color, or handicap, most will not fantasize about having a child who is dirty, who has lice-infested hair, or who wears ragged clothes.

The mothers responded positively to the appearance of the majority of the children in our sample. Some children, however, received a negative response because of the poor condition in which they were presented to their mothers. The biological mother who has a child with a defect, or a premature infant who looks "puny," or even a child of the "wrong" sex, may have some difficulty in bonding to that child. It is likely, then, that the adoptive mother who gets a "negative" first impression of her child may have an even more difficult time in bonding with the child.

Mothers gave a wide variety of descriptions of their first encounter examples, including:

1. Thrill/Joy/Happiness (64 responses): This category comprises responses of unqualified joy and happiness, such as, "It was love at first sight," "I was flooded with joy," "I just reached out and held her; it seemed so natural."
2. Disappointment (18 responses): The responses in this category were negative and often quite dramatic: "That can't be my child—oh, no!" "I felt trapped," "I felt my life was over!" "I felt my heart sink."
3. Mixture of Joy/Happiness and Fear/Anxiety (39 responses): Responses in this category were ambiguous. They were generally positively-toned but with some fear and insecurity evident: "I was full of fear, but also hopeful, happy, and scared." "I was anxious, but hopeful too." "I was thrilled, but also fearful whether I could handle it."

4. Frightened/Uneasy/Awkward/Inadequate. The mothers responding in this way described their first encounter experiences
as feelings of unease, helplessness, inappropriateness, or of not
being prepared to cope with the situation. Comments such as:
"He looked alien, not mine," or "I couldn't wait to get her out of
the agency and home," are typical.

Many descriptions of the first encounter experience were fairly
unique to the individuals making them. Several mothers felt distant
or detached from the experience. "I went through it feeling numb and
as though it were happening to someone else. I felt like an on-
looker." Others felt that the encounter was destiny or fate. Some of
these mothers spoke of a "sign" which indicated to them that this
was their child. "I knew she was meant for us when she started to
finger a piece of jewelry I was wearing. After that I relaxed more. I
felt I had my sign that she was our child."

Two aspects of bonding theory relative to the At Entry phase
seem to be supported by our findings—the mother's perceptions of
how much she was in control of the situation and the discrepancy
between the real and ideal child. The less able to cope with the situation a mother felt, the more negative did she perceive the first encounter experience. Also, the more she found her child to be different
from her expectations, the more negative was the experience. The
reactions of others accompanying the mother to her first meeting with
the child were also factors in how the mother responded to the child
and how she was able to cope with the situation.

Time 3: After Entry

In both biological and adoptive parenting, the situation becomes
more complex once the child or infant enters the family. The interaction between mother and child is now the focus, with mother and
child both bringing unique characteristics to that interaction. Even an
infant has a great effect on the quality of the interaction and thus on
the bonding which may occur. On the mother's side, successful con-
tributions to the interaction include verbal and non-verbal communication to the infant, nurturing the infant, claiming or identifying

the infant as part of the family, and working out a harmonious routine of interaction. As for the child, a newborn contributes to a successful interaction by communicating in some manner to the mother, by responding positively to her nurturing, and by behaving in a manner that elicits positive responses from her. The infant must adapt his inborn rhythms to establish a harmonious routine with the caretaker. The personality of the infant or child produces a unique pattern of interaction with the primary nurturer. Each mother-infant pair will attach or bond differently, depending on their characteristics. How much more complex is the process of interacting when the child has a background and history, as is the case when parents adopt an older child? Obviously, the older the child, the more history that child will have, and the more complex the bonding process becomes. In addition, environmental factors such as stressors and supports may affect the interaction.

We will now look at those factors which our sample of mothers found fostered closeness with, or produced distance from their child.

Closeness Factors

When asked, each mother mentioned several factors which helped her feel close to her child. Two major closeness factors emerged from responses. The first was physical closeness (68 responses). This included touching, hugging, holding, kissing, dressing, and feeding activities (nurturing activities varied with child's age). "I felt close to her when I fed and bathed her, and held her close to me." "I felt she needed me when she cuddled up to me, wanting to be held."

The second factor was "doing things together" (59 responses). These activities included cooking, traveling, doing household tasks, shopping, playing games, and visiting family and friends together. "We got closer when we went camping together." "I love music and my daughter does too. We go to concerts together and this helps us become close." "We enjoy playing games together."

These two factors, physical closeness and doing things together, seem very much in line with attachment theories. Physical closeness and nurturing activities directed toward the child seem to be the cornerstones of bonding in both biological and adoptive situations.

"Doing things together" seems to indicate the incorporation of the adopted child into the family unit. It also implies pleasurable forms of communication between mother, child, and family, and the establishment of harmonious patterns of interaction.

Somewhat less frequent responses were also found. Some mothers felt close to their children when outsiders treated them like the child's mother, or the child treated them as a mother: "When the teacher acknowledged me as his mother;" "When my friends said, 'Oh, this is your daughter;'" "When she ran to me, arms outstretched, calling, 'Mommy.'" Public declarations of responsibility such as registering a child in school, or religious rituals such as a Bris, also facilitated feeling close for some mothers. Several mothers cited that caring for their child when he was sick or injured helped them feel close to the child: "I went into the hospital and stayed with him. I felt close right away. It took several weeks before he could take the plane ride home with me." Others mentioned pride in a child and/or his accomplishments as a closeness factor.

These less frequent responses also seem to fall in line with current attachment theory. Public declarations of responsibility for a child are notices to the world that the child is claimed by the family. Outsiders acknowledging an adoptive mother as a child's mother aids with the claiming process and verifies the maternal role. A child treating the adoptive mother "as a mother" signifies the child's positive response to the mother's nurturing activities and helps with bond establishment. A child who behaves in a manner which elicits a pride response in his mother strengthens the bond between them.

Distance Factors

Along with factors which fostered closeness in the relationship, most mothers could cite factors which made them feel distant from their children. When considering closeness and distance factors, however, it is important to remember the variable of social desirability and it is possible that, since the interview or questionnaire was done only once, which meant that interviewers and interviewees were strangers, the mothers may have emphasized the positive closeness factors and deemphasized negative distance factors. Although there was no lack of negative responses, some negative aspects may have been withheld. It is natural to try to give as good an impression as possible, especially to strangers.

The distance factor most often cited by mothers was behavior by the child that was destructive, manipulative, or very negative (61 responses). These behaviors include stealing, lying, setting fires, hitting other children, tantrums, and rages. "He started setting fires. I was terrified. I knew we couldn't keep him unless that behavior stopped." "He stole from my purse and from his brothers and sisters. We had locks on everything." "He had such rages. He'd tear down the drapes, break things, scream."

Children who tended to be detached or rejecting made some mothers feel alienated (21 responses). "She keeps to herself pretty much. I know she misses her foster family." "Sometimes she screams, 'I hate you,' and I feel hurt and angry." In some instances,

the child would not cuddle, smile, or respond positively to parental
efforts. Exhaustion, depletion of energy and resources, and conflicts
with other roles made many mothers feel distant from their children
(34 responses). "She required all my attention at first. I was worn
out, and I saw resentment growing in my husband and my other children."

Finally, several mothers cited anxiety reactions and panic as a
hindrance to attachment. Mothers with this response were those who
had adopted children clearly unlike them racially or ethnically. A
typical response was: "What have I done? Does this child belong
here?"

Again, factors producing distance between mother and child
seem to flow logically from bonding theories. Negative, destructive
behavior on the part of a child would be expected to elicit negative
responses on the part of the mother. It would also signal a disruption
of routines in the family. In addition, a child's failure to respond to
maternal advances by detached or rejecting behaviors would fail to
affirm the maternal role and the claiming process by the mother.
Thus, children's destructive, detached, and rejecting behaviors are
seen to be deterrents to bond formation when viewed in the light of
current theory.

The anxiety reactions and panic cited by several mothers in
response to adoption of a racially different child also appears to have
a base in attachment theory. The more difficult it is for a parent to
"identify" the child as belonging to and fitting in with the family, the
more difficult it is to "bind-in" that child. Finally, environmental
stressors of depleted time, resources, and conflicts with other roles
may produce exhaustion in the adoptive mother that results in her
distancing herself from the child.

Support Systems

Probably the environmental influence which most affects bond formation between mother and child—in both biological and adoptive situations—is the presence and/or absence of a variety of support systems. It was well documented in our sample that the support systems
a mother can develop during the three time phases of bond formation

will greatly influence her evolving relationship with her adopted child. Although 64 mothers in our sample felt that they received their greatest support from their husbands, 16 mothers stated that the adopted child produced marital stress. Such comments as, "At one point I felt I'd have to choose between my husband and son," were not uncommon. Eighty-six mothers mentioned extended family and friends as important support systems. Again, support was not universal. Several mothers said that they received no support from extended family and friends, who, in fact, opposed the adoption. Some families and friends went so far as to sever ties with the adopting mother. "When you are pregnant, everyone helps you; when you adopt, no one helps you," is how some adoptive mothers saw it.

Other support systems were available for adoptive mothers. Fifty-eight mothers mentioned that groups—either formally organized units or informal networks of adoptive parents—supplied much-needed support. The community in general (that is, neighbors, church, schools) was mentioned as supportive by thirty-seven mothers, while only six mothers perceived the community as non-supportive. "The teachers were eager to help us. They went out of their way to be supportive." "Our church was wonderful. We found such support and acceptance." "Our neighbors were interested and helpful."

In general, our total sample of mothers indicated that acceptance of and assistance from such traditional supports as spouse, family, and friends helped them to establish their mothering role and to feel close to their child. When the family and/or husband accepted the adoption and child, the mother often felt somehow "released" to parent the child. "I felt much better once the grandparents showed acceptance."

On the other hand, rejection of the child and/or of the adoption by significant others made mothering much more difficult. "Relationships with my husband's family have never been the same since the adoption. They don't really accept our child as part of the family."

Attitudes Towards Open Records

One relatively new environmental stressor is the controversy surrounding open adoption records. With both biological parent groups and adoptee groups seeking more openness in the adoption process, the issue of open records is sure to have an increasingly great effect on the bond a mother develops with her adopted child. In our sample, twenty-nine mothers stated unequivocally that their children had a right to obtain full information about their biological parents and that they would help them do this if necessary. Another sixteen said that, although they felt threatened by open records and would not like to use them, they also would help their children obtain this information. "I know it will upset me, but I'll do all I can to help with the search."

Nine mothers felt strongly that open records leading to contact with biological parents should not occur before age eighteen: ". . . . otherwise I'd be a glorified foster parent." While no mothers in the interview group stated that they opposed open records, twenty-two mothers in the questionnaire group did oppose the concept. Perhaps the lack of interviewer presence freed these mothers to express this feeling. Six mothers stated that there was no issue since their child already knew who the biological parents were. Finally, thirty-three mothers, all of whom had adopted children from foreign countries, said their children had no records and thus there was little chance of their being able to find their biological parents. This was typically said with relief, although several of these mothers said they supported the concept of open records. ("No records" means that the names and addresses of biological parents are unknown.)

While it seems that most adoptive mothers accept the concept of open records, attachment theory indicates that there can be some danger in a constant threat of intervention by a biological mother. Klaus and others have documented many times that a mother has great difficulty attaching to her child if she feels in danger of losing him. While Klaus observed blocks to attachment due to illness or defects in the child which might eventually end in the child's death, the situation is not unlike the situation which might occur with un-restricted open records. If a mother delays attaching to a child whom she might lose to death, might not a mother delay attaching to a child whom she might lose to a biological parent who may come to reclaim the child's love?

Agency Relationships

A factor which spans the three bonding time phases, and which seems to exert a great deal of influence after the child is placed, is the adoption agency through which the child is adopted. A parent's relation with the adoption agency can either produce much stress and become a block to bonding, or, conversely, may be a support for the parent, thus fostering bonding.

The majority of the mothers reported that they had adopted their children through agencies in the United States, and a smaller group had adopted through foreign agencies (see Table 5-6).

Table 5-6.   Sources of Adoption (Numbers of Children Adopted)

	Interview Group	Questionnaire Group	Total
Agency, USA	41	60	101
Agency, Foreign	31	21	52
Unspecified Agency	0	11	11
Private Source	11	3	14
No Answer	4	11	15
	87	106	193

Mothers' responses to the two questions dealing with their feelings about adoption agencies can be divided into three categories: positive, negative, and neutral. Forty-two mothers felt they had had a good relationship with their agency. "The agency was excellent—the adoption supervisor and I had many talks concerning placement." Eight mothers felt neutral about or distant from their agency, while five mothers said their agency was adequate. Some mothers in this group had adopted through a foreign agency. "I really had very little contact with the agency. We filled out the papers and went and picked her up. We were at the agency no more than fifteen minutes."

Negative responses to the adoption agencies came from twenty-three of the mothers. In eleven cases, the agencies had misrepresented the child to the family about age, intelligence, or physical defects: "I was never told my child was three grades behind in school—I'd told them I didn't want a retarded child. I couldn't deal with it." Other frequent complaints concerning agencies were:

1. Lack of notice and preparation time for the child's arrival: "I waited three years and then they called and said 'Come tomorrow.'"
2. Agency intrusiveness: "I resented all the probing, all the fitness questions and financial questions—biological parents don't have this."
3. Agency ability to remove a child: "I never told the social worker about the tantrums and problems for fear of losing the child."
4. Agency inflexibility: "When I asked questions about my child's background, I was told maybe she wasn't the right child for me. I stopped asking questions."

When the mothers were asked for suggestions on how to improve agency services, however, most gave no response. Of those who responded, twenty-seven felt the agencies should give parents more notice and preparation time before making placements. Ten mothers felt that agencies should give parents more instruction, counseling, and support in the post-placement period. Finally, ten mothers believed that agencies should treat parents in a more humane manner.

Transracial Adoptions

One issue often mentioned was that of transracial adoption. In our face-to-face interview group, all sixty mothers were white, so children having a different racial or ethnic background were non-Caucasian. Unfortunately, we did not ask the race of the mothers on the questionnaires, but since the questionnaire mothers described non-white children as different from themselves, we assumed that these mothers were white.

In general, most mothers were forthright and open concerning the potential problems of a transracial adoption. For instance, they often mentioned that they felt more comfortable with lighter colored children.

One positive aspect of transracial adoptions is the fact that the child's ethnic or racial differences require a true acknowledgement of the adoptive situation. These mothers could not fantasize that their child was a biological child. In general, responses from mothers who had adopted transracially were very positive in relation to their attachment to the children and to the support they received from others.

Monotropy

Monotropy was another important issue discussed by mothers who adopted two or more children simultaneously (frequently these were siblings) or in close succession. These mothers usually felt that one of the children was easier to bond to than the other. In addition, they sometimes felt that while they were attempting to establish a bond with the second child, they were putting the newly-formed bond with the first child in jeopardy. "I felt that I was deserting my older child when I adopted the second one." Mothers who adopted an infant and an older child reported an easier bonding with the infant. Some factors which the mothers reported as affecting the ease of bonding to a second adopted child were the child's age, sex, physical appearance, and health.

This provides verification of the monotropy principle discussed by Klaus and Kennell (1976). It would seem that adoptive, as well as biological mothers can only attach well to one child at a time. When two children are adopted simultaneously, the younger of the two seems to have the advantage in the "choice" for most easily bonded child. Similarly, several mothers reported difficulty in attaching to an adopted child during periods of loss; that is, loss of a child or other loved one. Such observations indicate that it is difficult to "replace" a dead biological child with an adopted child before grieving is complete. The lost person must first be mourned and put to rest before the mother has enough psychic energy to invest in bonding to a child.

How Mothers Feel About Adoption

Over and above factors which affected the attachment process at the Prior to Entry, At Entry, and After Entry time phases, mothers in our sample were requested to discuss their general attitudes towards adoption. Their replies yielded additional insights on what might foster or block bonding in the adoption situation.

Several mothers indicated more than one attitude toward adoption, especially if they had adopted more than once. The overwhelming majority of mothers viewed adoption as highly positive for both parents and children. Their reasons for these positive feelings included their feeling that adoption strengthened marital and family ties, their knowledge that the child was wanted and sought (its arrival was never an accident), and their belief that this was a real chance for the child to have a "better life." Some mothers (32%) also saw adoption as positive, but with problems. These mothers seemed fairly certain, however, that the problems could be resolved.

Seven (6%) mothers had negative attitudes towards adoption: "Knowing what I know now I'd never do it again." Interestingly, all these mothers had adopted children over age four. In addition, all of these children had emotional disturbances and some had physical handicaps as well—the "hard core" of hard-to-place children. These mothers mentioned being totally unprepared for the severity of their children's problems. "It was really a shock. We are quiet people, not used to violence." In addition, mothers mentioned uncertainty about their child's background and concerns about the child's future as reasons that they perceived adoption as negative. Both Caucasian and non-white children were among the children whose mothers had this negative response.

Similarity to Biological Parenting

Another issue that was often brought up by the mothers who had adopted infants was the similarity they saw between the biological and adoptive parenting situation. Again and again they said that they could not perceive how they differed from mothers of biological children in their relation to their child. This viewpoint gained validation from mothers who had had both biological and adopted infants: "I see no difference: I had them both ways—it's the same, really." These mothers felt that their adopted children were as much "theirs" as their biological children.

Overdoing Parenting

Some adoptive mothers expressed the belief that they had to parent far more successfully than their biological counterparts. This belief stemmed from several causes. First, to receive a child from an agency, the parent had to successfully compete with others vying for a child. Parents were forced to prove themselves—that they would be the best parents. Second, the agency focus on the "best interests of the child," or "what can these parents give the child?" also tends to foster parental overdoing. In addition, adoptive parents must compete with the child's biological parents—adoptive parents feel compelled to give the child a better life than he would have had with the biological parents. Finally, for some parents, parental "overdoing" was a real necessity due to the state of the child. Some handicapped or disturbed children do require parenting time, energy, and expense over and above the norm.

6

The Children's Responses

Because bonding involves both child and parent, we asked adopted children their views of the bonding process. This phase of the study was done after our study of mothers' responses.

We used questionnaires rather than interviews for this purpose because we believed that the presence of an interviewer might be perceived as threatening by both child and mother. The questionnaires were sent to parents who had been referred to us as having adopted children that were then at least ten years old. (Most of the children were drawn from sources other than our original sample of families.) The parents were asked to read all the questions on the questionnaire and to delete any they felt were unsuitable before asking their children to participate. We wanted to be certain that the children who did not know they were adopted would not find out through us, and we wanted parental consent to be freely given before the child became involved. Actually, no questions were deleted by any of the parents who gave permission for their children to participate. Some parents refused to let their children participate, however. "It's a sensitive subject and I'd rather she didn't get involved," or "I don't know how it would affect him, so I don't want him to do it," were typical responses. These responses were understandable, although these parents' reluctance limited our sample, as did our limiting the study to children who were ten or older.

We had a return rate of 26 percent for our questionnaire, receiving 33 responses from children ranging in age from 10 to 18. We hope that at some future time we can continue this phase of the study with a larger sample. (See Appendix for Questionnaire.)

Before considering the responses to the questionnaires, it may be useful to review bonding theory briefly as it pertains to the child. Studies of child growth and development emphasize the importance of continuity and security in parent/child relationships (Neubauer). Children who are adopted past infancy lack this continuity, and establishing feelings of trust and security are major tasks for them. The child's insecurity coincides with that of the adoptive parents during the early phases of the adoption, making support by others, such as extended family, especially important.

The emotional development of the child is of great long term significance. We described some of the characteristics of unattached children in Chapter 3. Attachment to at least one competent nurturing adult is essential in enabling the child to develop into a stable, emotionally healthy person. A child who has attached to such an adult is in a better position to attach to a new parent than a child who has never had this experience. In the latter category are many children who have had multiple placements in foster homes and children who have grown up in institutions. A study by Carol Hovey of twenty-two adopted children illustrates these issues. Thirteen of her subjects were from Korea and nine were from the United States. Hovey found that the number of the child's prior placements and the age of the child at pre-adoption placement were important in determining how well the child became attached to its new parents. She found that the children with the fewest attachment problems were adopted in infancy (5 weeks to 13 months). The group with the most severe attachment problems was made up of four children. Two of these were two

and a half years old and had experienced two placements each prior
to adoption. The other two were five years old and had spent all their
lives in orphanages. Those with attachment problems experienced
such symptoms as severe temper tantrums, rebelliousness, distract-
ability, and fear of separation.

The child who has not developed a sense of trust, who is disabled
in relating to adults and peers, and who exercises little control over
his or her behavior will have to accomplish a great deal of personal
growth after adoption. Initially, the insecurity of a new situation plus
grief at loss of the former home makes this period especially stressful
for the child. Gradually, the child must develop an ability to receive
and give love, to care for others, to control behavior, to share and
trust, and to assess others' needs and responses and adapt to them.
Because bonding involves the development of a close human relationship, it may be highly threatening at first for a child brought up in an
impersonal atmosphere.

It may be helpful to recall here the mothers' assessments of the
strengths and problems of adopted children. Foremost among the
strengths of children adopted at an older age were resilience, adapt-
ability, possession of survival skills, increased sensitivity to the needs
of those who are poor or suffering, and awareness of other life styles
besides that of upper middle-class Americans. Among the problems
cited by mothers of adopted children were: Uncertainty about ancestry, knowledge that their own mothers had relinquished them,
insecurity due to changes in parent figures, and having to deal with
such complexities as being of a different race from the parent and the
possibility of searching for a natural parent. These problem areas
were also mentioned by some of the children who responded to our
questionnaire.

Findings

Of the thirty-three children who completed questionnaires, nine were
boys and twenty-four were girls. The length of time since adoption is
summarized in Table 6-1.

Table 6-1.   Length of Time Since Adoption at Time Questionnaires
Were Completed

Time	Number of Children
9 months through 2 years	12
3 years through 5 years	12
6 years through 8 years	5
9 years through 11 years	3
12 years through 14 years	1

The ages of the children at time of placement are summarized in
Table 6-2.

Table 6-2.   Age at Time of Placement

Time	Number of Children
Birth through 2 years	5
3 years through 5 years	3
6 years through 8 years	9
9 years through 11 years	8
12 years through 14 years	8

Thus, the children who responded were heavily weighted toward
those who were over five years old at the time of placement.

The ages of the children at the time of the study are summarized
in Table 6-3.

Children who differed racially or ethnically from their mothers
were also represented in our group of respondents. Eight of them
stated that they look similar to their adoptive mothers and twenty-five
said they looked different from their mothers. Of the latter group, six
said they were Korean, six said they were black and white mixed,
three said they were black, and two described themselves as black/

Table 6-3.   Children's Ages at Time of Study

Age	Number of Children
10 years through 12 years	18
13 years through 15 years	11
16 years through 18 years	4

Oriental (black/Korean; black/Vietnamese). One respondent indicated American Indian ancestry. The remaining seven children described themselves as looking different, in terms of skin tone and/or eye and hair color, from their mothers, but did not state their ancestry. Those children who described their mothers said their mothers were white.

Here are some answers to our questions:

What is it like to have a mother who looks different from you?

The responses to this were quite varied. Twelve children said, "I never think of it," or "I don't think about it." Three children gave no answer. Eight said, "It doesn't matter to me." Three of these children added comments such as, "If she were green, it wouldn't matter. She's still my mother." Two said, "I don't know." Some of the children who initially responded with, "I never think of it," or, "It doesn't matter," or, "I don't know," went on to add such comments as:

"It's the same as having a mother who looks like me."
"Sometimes I feel a little out of place."
"Sometimes I feel different."
"It's OK."
"I feel mad and sad."
"It's neat but different."
"It doesn't matter to me, but others keep asking me why I don't look like my mother."
"All children look different from their mothers."
"It feels strange."

Since looking racially or ethnically different from one's mother is hardly usual, it is surprising that so many of the children either said that they never thought about it or that it didn't matter to them. Although we may speculate that suppressing feelings about these physical differences is a way of coping, and also that some children may not have felt free to describe their views, comments by several children demonstrate that issues of race and ethnicity *can* be transcended in favor of the much more fundamental need of having a mother. "I know what it's like without a mother."

If you were old enough at the time of your adoption to think about it, did you imagine what your new mother would look like?

The responses to this question were related to the previous question on looking similar to or different from their mothers. Ten children said they had had fantasies of what their adoptive mother would look like. "Fat, curly, blonde," one child said, and another said, "Grouchy and mean looking." Four gave no description. Several children had fantasized a mother who looked like them and were disappointed when this was not the case (all of these children were Korean or Vietnamese). "I felt sad. She was not my Korean mommy."

Did she look the way you thought she would? Different?

One child gave no answer to this question, one said she was like the mother she had fantasized, and eight said she was different. Since among nearly all of the children who had fantasized, the actual adoptive mother was different from the fantasized mother, these children had to deal with a discrepancy. Only three children said they had had a realistic idea of what their adoptive mothers would look like. Of these, one had seen the mother before placement and two had seen photographs of their future mothers.

Fourteen of the thirty-three children said they had had no fantasies about their adoptive mothers. "No, I didn't think about it." Since most of the children giving this response were old enough to remember the period just prior to placement, we may assume that they, like many adoptive mothers, suppressed fantasy in an anxiety-laden situation. This suppression denied them the opportunity, which fantasy could have provided, of preparing themselves psychologically for meeting their new mothers.

The implications of these findings are that children need help in preparing, as realistically as possible, for meeting the new mother through such measures as pictures, letters, and descriptions of the mother and the family. After placement, children need assistance in verbalizing what they expected, in what ways the situation was similar to or different from their expectations, and whether they experienced disappointment. For example, those Korean children who expected a "Korean mommy" faced the task of grieving for that fantasized mother and accepting the actual mother.

Were you old enough to remember how you felt when you first met your new mother? If so, describe how you felt then.

Two children described themselves as feeling happy and excited about meeting their adoptive mothers. Seventeen said they felt scared, shy, and strange. Four described feeling mad and sad. Seven said they couldn't remember, as they were too young when they were adopted. Three other responses were:

"I had mixed feelings: happy and sad."
"I was glad to get out of an institution."
"I was glad my family didn't care what color I was."

Unlike adoptive mothers, for whom the first encounter was predominantly a time of joy and happiness, or a mixture of joy and apprehension, the first meeting with the adoptive mother was for most of these children a fearful event producing much insecurity. In addition, several children described poignantly their grief at leaving foster parents or orphanages—"I cried all night."

These findings can lead us to question the use of some words very current in relation to adoption. The adopted child, regardless of age, is typically told he or she is going "home" at placement. This choice of words is inaccurate from the perspective of the older child although it may be an accurate description of the parents' view. Clear, direct, and unambiguous language is a help to anyone in stress, and it is important to recognize that the adoptive placement is initially not "home" to the child past early infancy who must break previous attachments and adapt to strange surroundings. It is important for mothers to remember that what often is a day of intense happiness for them may be remembered by the child as an occasion of anxiety, insecurity, and possibly even terror.

Rather than being told what to feel, children being prepared for adoption need opportunities to express what this experience is like for them. "This is the happiest day of your life," "This is your lucky day," "Don't be scared," all serve to lessen the child's opportunities to describe his feelings about the experience. Adults who have worked very hard and incurred great expense to arrange for the adoption may find it hard to realize that the actual placement is frequently not a joyful experience for the child. Talking about the naturalness of fearing a new environment and a new family can help the child avoid feeling guilty or ungrateful toward those who are trying to help him.

Describe what helps you develop a relationship with your mother.

The responses to this question were highly individual and hence hard to summarize. To give their full flavor, all of them are included below. Some children gave more than one response to this question.

"When she takes me on vacation." (2)
"When she helps me get ready for school." (2)
"When she kisses and hugs me." (1)
"Talking with her and helping her." (2)
"When we talk and do things together (cook, play ball)." (4)
"Talking with her." (4)
"Telling her the truth about what goes on the rest of the day when she is not with me." (1)
"I realized I needn't be afraid of her." (1)
"Doing what she expects me to, and her treating me the way I like to be treated." (1)
"Buying me ice cream, and taking me to my art audition." (1)
"Going to New York City with her." (1)
"I know I'll be loved in spite of what I do." (2)
"I don't know." (2)
"When something goes right." (1)
"She helps me when I need help." (3)
"Sharing good times and sad times together." (1)
"My mother caring for me." (2)
"I liked being able to call her mother." (1)
"When she gives me privileges." (1)
"Mother sits and talks with me when I'm upset." (1)

"She is nice and loving." (1)

"She is patient." (1)

"Going places alone with her." (1)

"Discussing my past experiences with her without fear and hesitation; not worrying she'll think bad of me because I'm not perfect. (1)

No answer. (1)

Describe what gets in the way of developing a relationship with your mother?

"Nothing." (6)

"My foster mother told me I'd be a slave." (1)

"I don't think about it." (1)

"When I get in trouble." (1)

"Brothers and sisters." (5)

"I don't know." (1)

"I loved my foster mother and I didn't want anyone to take her place; I was afraid of losing my foster mother." (1)

"I didn't want to love my new mother or trust her because I might lose her again." (1)

"When my mother won't let me do what I want." (2)

"Sometimes I think abut my Korean family and I want to think about them and not about being an American." (1)

"Not knowing the language when I first came." (1)

"When I talk back." (2)

"When she jokes and teases." (1)

"When she turns the channel on a good TV program." (1)

"I do not like to talk; also, she might not know how to take care of my hair." (1)

"Peer pressure not to relate to her views and ideas. Maybe I was prejudiced against her." (1)

"When she punishes me." (1)

No answer. (4)

Describe times when you began to feel close to your new mother.

Answers to this question closely paralleled the answers to what helps develop the relationship, as would be expected.

"Sitting on her lap, holding." (2)

"When mother is in a good mood." (1)

"When I'm in a good mood." (1)

"When I started going to school about two weeks after adoption." (1)

"When I work on the farm." (1)

"She talks with me when I'm upset or angry." (2)

"A couple of weeks after adoption." (1)

"My relationship with my mother is closer than my friends' relationships with their mothers." (1)

"My mother works hard for us and does nice things for us." (1)

"When she took me out for dinner." (2)

"When we began to do things and go places together." (3)

"When I was here a year I began to feel close." (2)

"When I started meeting my mother's friends and family and was accepted as part of the family." (2)

"When she takes care of me when I'm sick." (1)

"It took about a month. My mother hugged me. Nobody ever hugged me before." (1)

"My mother was strict and made sure I didn't hurt myself." (2)

"When I was trying to teach her Korean words and we'd laugh because she couldn't say it right." (1)

"My first birthday with her." (1)

"When we were together at the hotel, waiting for my papers to come through so I could go to the U.S.A." (1)

"When I realized I was not such a bad person after all. When I realized my mother also did bad things when she was young." (1)

"When I knew she loved me even when I was bad." (2)

No answer. (3)

Describe times when you felt distant from your new mother (angry, annoyed, uninterested).

"When I ran away." (2)

"When I got in trouble." (3)

"When she needles me about my work." (1)

"When she tells me to do things I don't like (homework, chores)." (8)

"When I'm annoyed." (3)

"When she spanked me." (1)

"When I couldn't speak English and she couldn't understand me." (1)

"When I was homesick for Korea and I'd get mad at her very easily." (1)

"When she yells at me." (1)

"When I get upset." (1)

"I feel distant all the time." (1)

"My brothers and sisters make me feel distant." (2)

"When I didn't get my way." (1)

"When I was punished." (2)

What do you think are good things about being adopted (things you like)?

Children's responses varied widely, but on the whole they were very positive. Only two children said there is nothing positive about being adopted; four gave no answer. The remainder of the children had positive comments, which are summarized below. (One child gave two answers.)

"We go a lot of places." (1)

"You have something to be very proud of." (1)

"Being with a large family." (1)

"Having a permanent loving home." (2)

"Having someone or people to care for me." (1)

"Learning to love and trust and also give." (1)

"I am happy. I like to be in this family." (2)

"Someone cared for me and adopted me." (2)

"Good to have a Mom since my Mom died." (1)

"A lot of good things in it." (1)

"Having a parent and feeling someone loves me." (1)

"You will always have loving parents." (1)

"I like it because I have my own family." (2)

"I have a new home." (1)

"If I wasn't adopted I wouldn't be raised as well." (1)

"When you have a home, they can help you with your problems." (1)

"I know how it is without a mother." (1)

"I like being adopted." (2)

"Having a house to live in." (1)

"I think it's very good because children who don't have any mother can get one." (1)

"Gives children a home and clothes and food and love so they don't die. I think a lot of people should adopt children." (1)

"My new home; not having to move anymore." (1)

"I appreciate my mother much more than if I hadn't been adopted." (1)

Mothers in the study spoke little about their children's possible appreciation of the changes in their lives since adoption. Some mothers indicated they felt their children didn't remember their preadoption life, or didn't appreciate the change, or had become so accustomed to middle-class American ways that they had forgotten what it was like before. Children's answers to the question about adoption gave a different picture. Some children indicated that they were vividly aware of what adoption has meant to them, and that they appreciated the positive changes in their lives. Perhaps children feel less free to voice these thoughts amid the routines of their present lives. Reading their responses gives a clear impression of children who know something besides their current life situations and who are very aware of the fundamentals—"Feeling I belong to someone who loves me."

What do you think are bad things about adoption (things you don't like)?

Thirteen children stated that nothing is negative about adoption. Only one child said he did not like anything about being adopted. Four gave no answer. Other responses were:

"I don't like being punished." (1)

"Having to behave." (1)

"I can't have any pictures of myself when I was little." (1)

"I miss my Korean family." (3)

"The times when I say they are not my parents." (1)

"When other people don't like adopted kids then I feel unwanted and different." (2)

"English is hard." (1)

"They might not know how to take care of my hair and other things." (1)

"It's a bother when people ask why my parents are white and I'm not." (1)

"Some people make fun of me because I'm Oriental." (1)

"It is scary." (1)

"Sometimes I worry about my other parents. But I know I could find them if I really wanted to." (1)

Were you old enough to remember your social worker?

Most of the children in the sample could remember their social workers. Twenty responded "yes" to this question, while thirteen said "no." Those who answered no said either that they were too young to remember (8) or that they had had no social worker (5). Of the twenty children who could remember their social workers, ten described being well prepared for adoption by them, nine said they had either not been prepared at all or had been poorly prepared, and one child stated he could remember but preferred not to answer the question. Typical of the descriptions of positive preparation were:

"I had a lot of social workers. They helped me a lot. The best one got me a home."

"I was very well prepared. I got to meet my mother first."

"I was well prepared. My social worker took me alone and talked to me. He told me my new family were neat people and liked sports."

"She told me they have kids that play sports and not to get scared to go to a new home."

"My social worker got very close to me. I trusted her. I knew she would not send me to anyone mean."

Typical descriptions of poor preparation were:

"I did not know anything about my new family. I wish I had known ahead of time that I was going to America, the name of my family, and whether I'd have brothers and sisters."

"No, I was not well prepared. She screwed it up."

"A lawyer came to the orphanage to ask if I wanted to be adopted. I had no information about my family. Pictures and letters could have helped me a lot."

Thus, as even this small sample of thirty-three children shows, much remains to be desired in preparing children for adoption. The lack of preparation of mothers has already been discussed in Chapter 5. The situation is made even more complex when neither child nor mother has been realistically prepared for the experience. When planned and careful preparation by a social worker is lacking, it may by possible for parents to initiate some preparation by sending pictures and stories about the family. Sometimes it is possible for parents to find an English-speaking person who also speaks the child's language who can communicate with both child and parents prior to adoption, even if this individual is not a social worker. Members of religious orders, physicians, and teachers sometimes meet this need. Preparing a child for adoption is especially likely to be problematic when the child is adopted from another country.

These responses of children give us a glimpse of the child's view of what it is like to relate to an adoptive mother, and what the experience of adoption means to them. The fact that the sample consists primarily of children who were adopted after infancy and who have had to deal with multiple placements and orphanages, adds to the poignancy of the responses and also illustrates that these children, and their mothers who gave consent, were primarily the ones to reach out and make the effort to share with and help others through participation in the study.

What else would you like to tell about your adoption?

This open question received no response from twenty children. Ten gave positive responses describing their situations. One child described mixed feelings about adoption, one gave a negative response, and one used the open question to give an additional description of her adoptive family. The large number of children who left this question blank probably reflects the inability of children, who are still developing cognitively, to formulate answers to an open question. (Mothers, in contrast, provided a good deal of information when responding to open questions.)

Some of the children's positive responses were:

"A black child being adopted in a white home is not bad at all."
"The most important thing I've learned is to be honest and work

things out. At first, I wasn't relating to my mother. Maybe I was prejudiced.''

"I don't think about adoption very often. My Mom's my Mom and my Dad's my Dad.''

"I got adopted by a wonderful family.''

"I have a nice mother who does nice things for me.''

"Adoption is fun, interesting. Most of all, it is loving, caring, sharing. I love it. Adoption is terrific.''

"Adoption is great.''

"Being adopted is a very wonderful thing that the Lord made it happen to me. It was a very scary experience because I didn't know how long it would last. Knowing I have people that really care for me and that I really care for is a very great blessing.' 'The child who had mixed feelings said:

"Sometimes I'm glad about adoption; sometimes I'm sad. Sometimes I like my Mom and sometimes I don't."

The negative responder said:

"I miss my old ways and I will always miss my real folk."

Summary

The implications of this aspect of the study are, of course, very tentative, due to the small sample size. Nevertheless, the children's responses were very frank and were probably less influenced by social conventions than adult responses would be. One may, of course, question the ability of children to respond to such questions. Our impression was that the children knew what they thought, whether or not they were able to clothe their thoughts in intellectual types of language.

7

Implications of the Study

What are the implications of our study for parents, health professionals, and society? An important finding is the overwhelmingly positive view of adoption expressed by most of our respondents, a finding which is especially noteworthy in light of the inclusion in our sample of many older children, handicapped children, and children whose race or ethnicity differed from that of their adoptive parents. Some of these adoptive situations were clearly high risk from the standpoint of bonding theory. Nevertheless, most mothers and children seemed to be coping well.

The current literature on parenting in our society indicates that it is a complex and difficult task. Adoptive parents take on all the usual problems of parenting along with the complexities of having children who are not born to them, who may be racially different from them, who may arrive in mid-childhood, and whose belongingness to the adoptive family is increasingly under question by various groups. Clearly, a great deal is being expected of these parents and children. As we conducted our interviews, we were impressed with the amount of dedication and effort being expended by the mothers in order to relate to, and lovingly care for, their children.

Although the number of children who responded to questions about bonding with the adoptive mother was small, those who did respond gave clear indications of their efforts to cope with such problems as past multiple placements, racial and social differences from adoptive parents, and dealing with the fact of adoption and the knowledge that their birth parents could not keep them. These children were, in addition, facing all the complex tasks of any child in our society. While many of the older children began their adoptive experience with deficits due to inadequate nurturance, they were nevertheless expected to cope, and in large part described themselves as coping, with these challenges. The resilience of these children and the perseverance of their mothers were striking. Several mothers indicated that, after an initial phase, their child simply and normally became one of the group at school and in the community, competing with other children who had more favorable early life experiences.

The most significant findings of our study support what theories of bonding would lead one to believe: that bonding is facilitated when the child is physically and emotionally healthy; that bonding with a child under two years is easier and quicker than with a child over that age; and that bonding with a child of similar race and ethnicity is easier than bonding with a child of markedly different race and ethnicity. These findings, however, are enmeshed in data which indicate that even though bonding is more difficult and slower when the child has a handicap, or is racially different, or is older, many satisfactions and rewards can come to parents who adopt such children. We are emphasizing the bonding process, not final results. It may be that families who must make extra efforts achieve a highly satisfying relationship with their children. Responses from mothers in the study indicate that this is true in many instances.

Mothers in our study expressed happiness and satisfaction in the mothering role. For those who already had other children, the role change was not so great. but for those who became mothers only through adoption, taking on the mothering role was felt to be a positive experience; many described it as the most satisfying event of their lives. "Real happiness," "Makes my life complete," "Thrilled," are some descriptions. Mothers who had never had children before described how friends, relatives, and colleagues quickly acknowleged them as mothers, enabling them to become part of "mother concerns" in various settings such as schools and parties. "It opened a whole new life to me—of children's books, music, art— all things I would have missed otherwise." "I was accepted by my friends as a mother right away." While the children were gaining, through love and care, improved nutrition, and vastly improved chances in life, their mothers' worlds were being broadened and enhanced. While a few mothers were disillusioned and would not do it again, the disillusionment had to do with their children's very severe handicaps rather than with their role as mother.

These positive outcomes are stressed initially because as we discuss implications we will emphasize less positive responses. As you read on, remember the findings described in the previous chapter which indicate that most mothers and children are thriving.

The Older Adopted Child

While the largest number of children (113) in the first study were adopted under the age of two, a significant number (80) were adopted over that age. Eighteen children in the study were adopted between ten and thirteen years of age. As would be expected, our respondents indicated that it took longer to bond with an older child than with an infant or toddler. Those mothers who had adopted both infants and older children were especially clear about the difference—"I felt the baby was mine right away," "As soon as I held him I knew he was my son"—while it often took a year or even longer to experience this feeling with an older child. The implication is that parents who adopt older children should be counseled ahead of time to expect the process to take considerable time. Some mothers in our study described severe loss of confidence when they did not feel immediate bonding to their child. Data from our study suggest that older children who have already experienced satisfactory mother-child relationships, either with a foster mother or birth mother, can relate more readily to an adoptive mother than children who have lived most or all of their lives in institutions or on the streets. In the latter groups, anxiety over close family relationships and lack of readiness to become involved manifested themselves in a good deal of disruptive behavior which sometimes persisted for months or even longer. Such difficulties may surprise the mother, as they run counter to her expectations that an extremely needy child will immediately show pleasure and gratitude, and will warm quickly to a welcoming environment.

A mother's expectations about bonding with her adopted child must be attuned to what is possible and likely, given the circumstances. Severe frustration and feelings of hurt and rejection on the part of the mother are understandable but do not help her to cope. These reactions can be tempered by learning before placement about the child's background and what he is probably able to bring to the relationship. Post-placement counseling and support are important, and should include the mother and the entire family as well as the child. The mother who realizes that it will take time for the child to relate to her, and who is not unrealistically caught up in slogans about instant love and forever families, is in a better position to deal with an older child than one who has unrealistic fantasies. Mothers in our study who had adopted older children who had been abused and deprived gave many touching accounts of the gradualness of relating, which typically occurred in sporadic breakthroughs of closeness and affection followed by setbacks and then further progress. One mother said, "One day when I was straightening up his room I suddenly realized how much he had been through and I sat down and cried. That day I couldn't wait for him to come home from school so I could hug him."

Contact with others who have adopted older children is especially helpful in keeping expectations realistic. It is hard to deal with a deprived and often angry and overly dependent child in the context of a middle class lifestyle and community. The child may not be ready at first for the give and take involved in scouting or church activities, or able to cope very well with social gatherings of family and friends. Situations likely to be especially difficult are those which are unstructured—for instance, where there is plenty of food, as at a party. While social expectations dictate a certain restraint in such a situation, a child who has never had enough to eat may, when confronted with a buffet supper, seem to take leave of his senses and begin heaping huge amounts of food onto his plate, into his mouth, pockets, and so on. Parents have to be prepared to alter their lifestyles temporarily so as not to place the child in situations which he cannot handle. Proceeding slowly and gradually with new situations and having a backup plan of what to do if the child cannot cope are important. When attending an informal dinner or gathering, it is wise not to make commitments to drive others home, so that one can leave promptly if necessary. Simply leaving when the child cannot cope is usually the best policy. It helps to remember that the child will gradually learn how to deal with such situations, and that it is best not to listen to well-meaning advice from those used to dealing with children socialized into families from birth, advice such as, "If you let him leave now, he'll always want to leave," and so forth. Although it may not be tactful to announce it, parents of adopted, deprived older children are dealing with situations which are not familiar to most other parents, and it helps to recognize this and to trust one's own judgment concerning the child's tolerance and one's own.

The child who already has many new experiences to deal with usually responds best to considerable structure and very clear expectations regarding behavior. One mother who had adopted several older children described the environment provided for the new child as "boot camp." She eased the rules and introduced flexibility as the child gained a greater sense of security and more self-control. She found that selecting one or two behaviors to work on with the child, rather than trying to deal with everything at once, was a help to both child and parent. Thus, selecting one aspect of personal hygiene to work on can help, but it means tolerating many other behaviors which the parent may feel tempted to try to change. The immensity of the changes already facing the child by reason of the adoption means that one must proceed slowly with changes, however desirable they may be.

Handicaps

The largest number of children in our first study had no handicaps reported by their mothers. However, a significant number (57, almost one-third) had some handicapping condition. Preplacement awareness of known handicaps is essential. It is easier to learn about the handicaps of an older child than about those of an infant only a few days old, whose disabilities may not yet have manifested themselves.

Some mothers in our study said they knew beforehand about their child's handicaps, while others either did not know because the information was not available or because it was withheld. In the latter instance, mothers spoke bitterly about being misled. It is likely that such bitterness makes relating to the child difficult. Agencies and private sources who so mislead parents (fortunately, a minority in our sample) may have no awareness of the harm that this can cause in a parent-child relationship. The expectations of the parents are important, too. It is relatively easy to be intellectually aware and accepting of a disability when it is discussed in a theoretical way, but one's emotional responses to a child's disability within the fabric of daily life are more complex. Also, a disability which seems minor in a developing country may seem major in a middle-class suburb in the United States. Thus, what at first appears to be deception may reflect different standards of assessment. All parents, whether biological or adoptive, must face the possibility that their child will be handicapped. However, the element of possible deception must be a concern for adoptive parents, since those placing the child for adoption have prior knowledge of the child which may not be entirely shared with the adoptive parents.

Standards of health care vary widely in different parts of our country and different nations of the world. Very high standards of medical and dental care are expected of middle-class parents in the United States. A child who has never seen a dentist in the first seven years of life may not only be having cavities filled soon after placement, but may be having an orthodontic evaluation. These differences in standards often mean large initial investments of time and money and care in an effort to treat health problems which might never have occurred in a more benign environment. It is important for people seeking to adopt to consider how they will feel about making up for past neglect if this process becomes costly and difficult. Whenever feasible, it is desirable for parents to have their own pediatrician assess the situation prior to placement. What one parent can do with joy and commitment, another may find draining and a cause for resentment.

While most of the mothers, including mothers whose children had handicaps, were enthusiastic about adoption, a few stated that, knowing what they know now, they would not do it again. In every instance, these were mothers of children with multiple handicaps. In contrast, some mothers in our study who had very disabled children were optimistic and coping very well. Those mothers who had a clear understanding of the disability and what it entailed prior to placement were those who gave the more positive responses. Those who were taken by surprise, and especially those who were misled, held the most negative views. All mothers reporting that their children had serious emotional problems had adopted their children over the age of four. It is important to note, however, that some children in the study who were adopted after age four were described by their mothers as emotionally stable and well adjusted.

There is, of course, a great element of chance involved in adoption. One mother adopts a six-year-old who is emotionally stable and quickly establishes a loving relationship with him. Another mother also adopts a six-year-old who requires years of psychotherapy and special schools, and who creates turmoil within the family. Chance operates also in biological parenting, but it is not as risky as the adoptive situation where the details of the child's past life are often unknown. Those who adopt must be able to cope with risks, and must find ways to gain the support and help they need during this process.

In his book, *In the Belly of the Beast*, Jack Abbott gives a searing picture of what it is like to grow up without a permanent home. Abbott was moved to many different foster homes during infancy and childhood. Finally, during adolescence, he was placed in a state correctional facility due to his failure to adjust to life in foster homes. From then on, his life was one of crime and imprisonment. He was paroled, and shortly thereafter was accused of homicide. Abbott believes the circumstances of his childhood stunted the growth of his conscience, sense of responsibility, and ability to care for and about others, and that it left him with chronic rage.

Adoption cannot solve all problems, but it can help some children. It is helpful to remember that each child's life is as important to him as ours is to us. Each child who is removed early enough from a series of foster placements, from an institution, or from wandering the streets has a better chance to develop into a humane, caring, responsible person. When considering the results of neglect, we can question why many prospective parents continue to be refused the opportunity to adopt, despite some recent increased flexibility in the selection of parents.

Racial and Ethnic Differences

The largest number of children in our first sample were white (about 39%). However, if we add together the children who were black (2), black and white mixed (34), Hispanic (34), Oriental (43), and American Indian (4), we have a total of 117 non-Caucasian children (61%). The degree to which these children resembled their adoptive parents differed greatly. Some Hispanic children with very light complexions blended easily into their communities, while others with darker skins did not. Since all the mothers whom we interviewed were white and those answering the questionnaire gave data indicating they were white, the issue of transracial adoption was an important one in our study.

A few mothers, as was noted previously, had brief panic reactions after bringing home a non-white child. These reactions were described as transitory and as occurring very soon after placement. All but three mothers who adopted transracially described their relationships with their children as satisfactory, and most described them as very good.

Many of the mothers who adopted non-white children described initial problems with extended family which lessened once the child arrived and direct relationships were established between the child and extended family and close friends. Three mothers, however, said that their adoption of a non-white child led to completely terminating an important relationship (family or close friend). In one of these instances, the child was of black/white mixed race and in two instances the children were Oriental. Simon and Altstein, in their follow-up study of transracial adoption (1981), noted that seven years after adoption, 12 percent of the families continued to have rifts in their relationships with extended family, while the remainder of the respondents indicated that the adoption did not change their relationships with extended family.

Community responses were described by most mothers in our study as supportive and positive toward interracial adoptions. Schools, churches, and neighbors were perceived as helpful and friendly. However, even in our small sample of thirty-three child respondents, some of the children described experiencing some difficulties at school and in the community due to racial issues. We may speculate that parents may not always be aware of the pressures their children are facing, or may try to minimize the difficulties. It is also possible that members of the community extend support to the mother which they do not extend to the child. All the children responded in terms of positive coping—"I have learned not to pay any attention to bigots. I just go ahead with what I am doing."

In contrast with our results, Simon and Altstein found that, while relationships with neighbors were initially reported as good, seven years after transracial adoptions only six percent of respondents indicated that these relationships were good. Simon and Altstein attribute this to the fact that the children had grown older, were possibly more assertive, and were certainly more visible. Many of the non-white children in our study were older, but the parents' assessments of neighbors' reactions were much more positive than in Simon and Altstein's study.

The extent to which transracial adoption is helping to find homes for waiting non-white children in the United States is negligible. Figures from the Department of Health, Education and Welfare in 1975 (the last year for which these statistics are available) indicate that black and mixed-race (black/white) children represented eleven percent of all adoptions in the United States. Of that figure, only .08

percent were adopted transracially. Our sample of thirty-six (19%) black and black/white mixed adoptions by white parents is, therefore, exceptional. Unfortunately, we did not have responses from black families, who constitute the largest potential source of adoption of black and mixed-race children.

While a large proportion of waiting children in the United States are school age black and mixed-race children, many agencies have changed their policies since 1975 to preclude transracial adoption.

Some mothers in our sample who had adopted overseas stated that they undertook the expense and risks of foreign adoptions because they felt they could not accept a black or racially mixed child.

Mothers in our study who had adopted transracially frequently mentioned that a positive aspect of their situation was the necessity to confront and deal with the fact of adoption. It was not possible for these mothers or children to deny that the children had been adopted. Since hiding adoption from a child or others is widely recognized as conducive to difficulties for the child later when the situation must be confronted, this was fortunate.

Because of racial polarization in housing, most of our respondents lived in all white neighborhoods. However, many indicated that they were making an effort to provide a racially integrated environment for their children by their choice of schools and churches. None of the respondents who adopted transracially mentioned moving to a different neighborhood in order to provide a more racially integrated environment. An unpublished study by Dr. Ruth McRoy of the University of Texas emphasizes the importance for transracially adopted children to have contact with a racially integrated environment. Her study stated that children in racially integrated situations function better than those who lack such contact.

In responding to the question, "What else would you like to tell me?" many mothers who had adopted Asian and South American children viewed it as likely that when their children were grown they would be living in communities similar to those of their adoptive parents. Those who had adopted black and white mixed race children were less sure about where their grown children might live. If longitudinal studies are carried on in the future, they will shed light on these concerns. At present, the cohort of transracially adopted children placed in the late 1960s and early 1970s are in late childhood and early adolescence, and therefore it is too early to assess the long-range implications for the families involved.

All mothers in our study who had adopted transracially stated that their nuclear families had become more accepting of racial differences since the arrival of the non-white child. These mothers said it was broadening and healthy for all members of the family to have children of other races visiting as playmates. An interesting finding in the study of Simon and Altstein is that transracially adopted children have positive self-images and that they are remarkably free of racial prejudice.

We may speculate that any change in ascribed roles and relationships may be threatening to some members of both races. Seeing a child and parent who are obviously affectionate and thriving but who are of different races may evoke tenderness and helpfulness in most people, but for some it may be a threat.

Fantasies

Data on fantasies was particularly interesting, and we turn now to the implications of our finding that fantasy is suppressed among many adoptive mothers, and that our respondents related this suppression to fears and uncertainties of what the child would be like, insufficient time between notification of the child's availability and a request to come for the child, and fears that, through some unforseen circumstance, the child may not really become available.

Measures that can free the mother to engage in the normal process of fantasizing in preparation for her new child are important. Notifying parents who have waited for years for a child to "pick him up tomorrow" does not allow them time to fantasize about, and prepare for, the child. In contrast, if the parents are given the opportunity over a reasonable period before adoption to have the child's picture to look at and think about, and to learn about the child's size and age and something about his background, they will have time to develop realistic, positively-toned fantasies, thus helping them prepare to bond with the child. Nesting behaviors help in practical ways as well as in stimulating fantasy. Mothers' accounts of hurrying to a neighbor to borrow a few clothes are common in our data, and are in sharp contrast to others who had time to shop for their child's clothing, thus preparing themselves through their feelings of expectation and their fantasies ("Will she look nice in this pink dress?") to receive the child.

The other two factors cited by our respondents as interfering with fantasy are less amenable to change. Adoption in the United States deals with older chidren, handicapped children, and racial minorities. Those who seek to adopt, therefore, are subject to anxieties about the kind of child who may be placed with them, and since the process can miscarry, they are also subject to fears that the adoption may not take place. Such anxieties can be mitigated somewhat by careful and honest discussions about the type of child the parent is willing to accept and the likelihood of finding such a child. No respondents in our sample who adopted from agencies in the United States stated that the adoption miscarried at the final stages. This fear, while natural, was unfounded for that group of mothers. A few respondents who adopted children overseas had this unfortunate outcome, but in all instances they were able to retrieve the situation in some way and finally succeeded in adopting a child. Some of our respondents described flying to meet their child in another land only to find the child extremely ill and in immediate need of hospitalization or severely malnourished to the point of illness. In one instance, a mother travelled to meet her child only to find that the child had already died. Another child was found for her, but the woman faced the difficulty of mourning her original child while bonding to a new child. Standards of cognitive, physical, and emotional assessment are very different in the developing countries from those in the United States, making uncertainties very real.

Since our data shows that most mothers fantasized a healthy child who would be racially and ethnically similar to them, another implication of our study is that some adoptive mothers will be disappointed initially, and that they will need to mourn the loss of the idealized child in order to bond more effectively with the child who is theirs. This suggests the need for increased post-placement services which focus not just on the child but also on the mother and the entire family. It is much easier for a parent to think positively about an unknown child's handicap, race, or ethnicity than to cope with them in reality.

Post-Placement Services

A major implication of our study, and one articulated by many mothers in our sample, is that there is a need for more and improved post-placement services, including group and individual counseling of children and parents. Groups of adoptive parents were seen as particularly helpful in providing such services because of their involvement with and understanding of the issues concerning adoption; because families often find the fees of private psychotherapists prohibitive, particularly over an extended period; and because the extended family sometimes requires time to adapt before its members can offer support. Some adoptive parents' groups offer hot lines which are especially useful for those with newly adopted children and children encountering many problems. Several mothers commented that services should encompass all members of the immediate family and not just the adopted child, since all members are usually experiencing stress. Although the adoption agencies could be sources of support and counseling, they were usually mentioned by our respondents with reservations and ambivalence due to the conflict between the power of the agency to remove the child and the parents' need to confide concerns and problems. The need for neutral persons to provide counseling and guidance is clear. Public health nurses and nurses in private practice may be able to offer such a service due to their familiarity with issues of child rearing and family relationships. Clergymen may also provide help, particularly if they have an orientation toward pastoral counseling.

The need for post-placement services was especially noticeable among those who had adopted foreign born children. If a child is adopted overseas, there is currently no agency mechanism for follow-up as there is among adoption agencies in the United States. Because of the high incidence of health problems among these children and the culture shock they must undergo, it is very important to provide post-placement services to them and their parents in an organized fashion.

The First Encounter

The first encounter between mother and child was described vividly and with much feeling by all our respondents. The frequently repeated comment, ''It was a never-to-be-forgotten experience,'' was illustrated repeatedly as we listened to or read very detailed accounts of the first meeting. The feelings were overwhelmingly positive for most mothers, while for a few there was disappointment, bewilderment, or a sense of unreality. Most mothers described a sequence of a build-up of excitement, suspense and anxiety before meeting the child, followed by relief at actually seeing the child coupled with a strong wish to get away from the agency, airport, or wherever the first meeting was occurring. With younger children, it was typical for mothers to undress and look at the child and then dress him in new clothes as quickly as possible. Reactions to the child's appearance, fears (''Is he really mine?''), and looking to others for support were common. In reviewing these accounts of the first meeting, it is clear that some mothers had, in however non-traditional a way, the support so important for bonding. They were accompanied by their spouse, parents, or close friends. They went to an agency where they had already established a relationship and, in some instances, they had had the opportunity to visit the child or have the child visit them before the final placement. All mothers described a feeling of relief after getting the child away from the agency and into their own care, and this relief was emphatically linked to the mother's feeling that the child was finally hers. Uncertainty about whether there would be a child and whether the mother could have that child persisted until departure from the agency. This reaction again reflects the problematic nature of the agency's role: to help and counsel, but also to have power to remove (or withhold) the child. One mother gave a description which was quite typical. "I had a cold. I was afraid not to go for fear they would give my baby to someone else. But I was also afraid I might cough, and then they might not give me the baby because of that."

Mothers who adopted foreign children and whose children were accompanied on the trip to the United States by stewardesses, described going to a huge airport, waiting among crowds, and hearing a stewardess calling out last names and guiding each child or handing each infant to the parent whose name was called. Although exciting, such a scene is hardly supportive and presents many problems of noise and confusion. One mother said, "I just never thought it would be done that way—just a name called on a list. We took our child and left, and that was it."

In view of the importance ascribed to this first meeting by our respondents and by the literature on bonding, it is essential to develop procedures for dealing with this first encounter. While those who adopt through agencies in the United States usually have substantial prior contact with agency personnel, those who adopt overseas may have only a very brief contact with an adoption agency. (Some parents who adopt children from foreign lands do so through agencies in the United States, while others deal directly with agencies overseas.) It seems important to counsel the mother to bring at least one other person with her—spouse, parent, close friend—at the time of placement to share the experience and to support her. This may not be feasible with foreign adoptions, where the parent's only contact with the agency may be at the time of placement, and where it may be necessary for the mother to remain in the foreign country for several weeks in order to complete necessary procedures, such a securing a passport for the child and dealing with immigration requirements. When children being adopted arrive at airports in the United States, it is necessary to have a room or at least a roped-off area where parents and children can meet apart from crowds and confusion. Since the child's initial appearance can crucially affect how the mother reacts to him or her, it is important for those accompanying such children to tidy them before arrival: a fresh diaper or, if the child was airsick, cleaning up the vomitus. In contrast with how the birth mother feels about the secretions of the baby who has just come from her own body, the bodily secretions of a child who is a stranger on arrival are not initially viewed as "mine" by the adopting mother.

Serious misrepresentation of the children presented problems for eleven mothers in our sample. These misrepresentations included describing a child who was clearly retarded as of normal intelligence, stating that a child who had a severe limp walked normally, and indicating that a child who was actually ten years old was five years old. While such experiences were in the minority, the mothers described feelings of shock, anger, disbelief, and of being misled. Such feelings cannot help but interfere with bonding with the child.

Our data and our study of the literature on bonding lead us to conclude that insufficient emphasis is being placed upon the way the first meeting with the child is handled. It is analogous to a biological mother's first contact with her child, a situation which is now receiving much emphasis in maternity care. Although specifics are different, adoptive mothers, too, need attention and support from caring others. They need some privacy as they first interact with their children. Having an opportunity for some reasonably relaxed interaction with the child immediately after the meeting is important. Parents who understand the importance of these factors when beginning the relationship with the child can make plans to have extra help at the time of placement so that the mother can be relieved of some of her tasks of cooking, shopping, and caring for other children in order to have time with the newly arrived child.

A leave from work for new biological mothers is accepted and, of course, has a biological as well as a socio-psychological basis. If we believe that socio-psychologic factors are important, then it is appropriate for adoptive mothers also to expect a paid leave of several weeks. Unfortunately, allowances for such leaves are the exception. Because adoption is a non-traditional way of having a family, it has been too easy for employers and others significant in the mother's life to view the occasion simply in terms of "picking up the child."

It is time to address the situation of the first meeting of mothers with their adopted children and their first weeks together with reference to what we know of bonding theory, and to use this theory to assist the mother and child to begin their lives together as smoothly as possible. Neglect of these considerations may have some relation to the competitive nature of adoption: perhaps it has been assumed that once one is lucky enough to have a child, one should ask for no more. Such an attitude belies current knowledge and may impede the bonding process.

Closeness and Distance Factors

Data from our study on closeness and distance factors affecting bonding with the new child are largely what would be expected in any mother-child relationship. Mothers who adopted infants spoke of holding, feeding, bathing, diapering, and cuddling the baby as important in bonding. Those who adopted older children emphasized doing things with them: cooking, shopping, traveling, camping, and so on.

A closeness factor that was different for our sample than what one would expect for birth mothers had to do with being acknowledged as the child's mother by teachers, neighbors, friends, and others. Mothers made comments like:

"It helped when I was accepted by all my friends as a mother. I just pitched in and helped with birthday parties and car pools. Overnight I had become a mother and my friends related to me that way."

"I felt very much his mother when I enrolled him in Sunday School and I gave my last name as his last name."

"When my child got hurt, suddenly I was a full-fledged mother, calling the doctor and being dealt with as his mother without question."

"When people saw me with him, they'd say he looks a little like me."

Interestingly, most of our respondents indicated that acknowledgment by others was immediate and definite, regardless of whether mother and child resembled each other. Recognition and support of the mother's role are very important in establishing her relationship with the child. We may conclude from our findings that either the mothers in our sample were exceptionally fortunate, or that most people are supportive of a child's finding a home and show this by promptly acknowledging the mother-child relationship.

Distance factors described by mothers related largely to children adopted past infancy. (A few mothers of infants spoke of a child's crying all night as a distance factor.) Lying, stealing, running away, physical violence, and setting fires are all examples of disturbed behavior in the unattached child (Cline). Such behavior was not typical of the majority of the children in our study, although the 31 emotionally disturbed children had problems at home, at school, and in their neighborhoods. Some mothers of these disturbed children reported withdrawal of initial support by others, such as teachers, neighbors, and friends. Indeed, few people in our society are willing to cope with severe emotional disturbance over long periods.

A crucial question becomes whether a nuclear family can persist in the face of such emotional stress. We became aware of only two adoptions in our sample which resulted in termination of the adoption. In both cases, the children were emotionally disturbed at adoption. One other child was placed in a residential facility for emotionally disturbed children. Since we have not done a follow-up study, we do not know whether other disruptions occurred subsequently.

A stalemating situation, described by several mothers of severely emotionally disturbed children, can also occur. These mothers had run dry in their efforts to help the child and to deal with the community on behalf of the child. "I've gone too far to give up, but I can't live with him either," said one mother, describing her stalemate situation. Prompt help from counselors, parents' groups, and schools which can give individualized attention is important. Some of the mothers had struggled alone for up to six months before seeking help, sometimes out of a feeling of failure, sometimes because they were so overwhelmed with trying to cope that they didn't have the energy to reach out. The mothers of these disturbed children described themselves as the child's main support, and had many tales of rejection by others: "I can't get a sitter to come. One time and that's it." "He can't go to camp. They won't have him." "She has no friends, not one. Even the roughneck kids have been told to stay away from her."

Even though a child is disturbed when he is adopted, the adopting parents are totally responsible from the time of placement in the sense of dealing with schools, playmates and others. Foster Cline's book, *What Shall We Do with This Kid?*, is an excellent resource. Cline emphasizes the importance of the first three years of life in the child's emotional development. He describes how the reliable gratification of meals accompanied by a sense of warmth and security with the mother locks the child into a pattern which enables him to trust others and himself, and to give and receive love. In the unattached child, there has been a disturbance in this essential cycle, and with each passing year the situation becomes harder to remedy, according to Cline. These children may become destructive of themselves and others, both physically and in terms of relationships. Cline emphasizes that the conventional methods suggested in various manuals and used by many parents, teachers, and therapists are ineffective with these children. Instead, Cline recommends highly confrontive techniques which reach through the child's manipulation and destructiveness and help him, as a result of the confrontation and its resolution, to feel security and love.

Exhaustion, depletion of energy, and conflict with other roles led thirty-four mothers in our study to feel distant from their children. Birth mothers experience similar problems. Providing for help within the home, if possible, and for periods of relief for the mother are important, especially for mothers of emotionally disturbed and physically handicapped children. Although the child's need for the mother's presence often seems insatiable, an exhausted and irritable mother is not prepared to cope with the child. Conveying to a demanding, manipulative child that one is exhausted or can no longer cope usually leads to an escalation of the demands and behavior problems. It is important to remember that, in our study, even mothers who felt overwhelmed and depleted expressed overall satisfaction with their roles as mothers. (Only six mothers, you may recall, were sorry they had adopted and would not do it again knowing what they know now.)

In responding to the question, "Did you experience the feeling of, 'Now he's my child?'" most mothers responded that the closeness developed gradually, rather than in a "this is it" kind of experience. However, some mothers who had adopted healthy infants had an immediate feeling of "This is my child."

Responses to our question about the positive aspects of adoption for the child indicate that adoption was viewed by all mothers as far superior to the alternatives of temporary foster homes or institutionalization. Most mothers viewed adoption as also positive for the mother. Several mothers pointed out that it would be preferable for the child not to have to go through the experience of knowing he was given up by birth parents, the uncertainty about ancestry, and the possibilities of a record search, all of which they viewed as further complicating the child's normal development. However, these mothers stated emphatically that once the child was in the situation of needing a home and care, adoption was the best possible solution. Some respondents emphasized that adopted children are survivors, that they have greater resourcefulness than the average child, and that they have quick compassion for those who are poor, hurt, and needy. However, although some of the children came to their adoptive homes from extreme privation, no mother reported a child having a greater than average appreciation of such benefits as food, clothing, and education. Apparently, children quickly accept middle-class standards and expectations as the norm.

These findings imply that parents should take responsibility for helping their children with issues of ancestry, loss of birth parents, and other factors related to their adoption by encouraging and initiating discussion and by helping the children prepare photo albums and scrapbooks about their past lives. Links with important persons from their past must be respected and contact maintained, if it is helpful to the child, by telephone, letters, and visits. Usually the urgency about these contacts slowly diminishes as the child becomes established in the new environment. Respecting and acknowledging the normal grief process the older child must go through for what he has left behind (however undesirable that past environment may seem to us) is important. Awareness of the culture from which they have come can be fostered among foreign-born children and may even be enhanced after adoption.

Many adoptive parents' groups also include children's activities. Experiences with other adopted children of all races and nationalities can help the child feel more "normal" and gain a wider perspective on adoption. One child, quiet for a long time during a ride home after a party for adopted children, said, "Mommy, are *all* these children adopted?" In another instance, a group of adopted children attended a birthday party. They represented three races and six nationalities. While the children ate cake and ice cream, they were asking one another, "Where do you come from?" "How long have you been here?" One child of six ran excitedly to her mother and said, "Mommy, where do I come from?" In the excitement she had momentarily forgotten she was from Colombia.

Children who look distinctly different from their mothers can be helped by having a previously discussed "story" ready to relate to casual inquiries. The child who is confronted several times daily with, "What, *she's* you mother?" can weather this better if not obliged to think through a response to each question. This does not imply that the issue is dealt with superficially at home.

If more than one child in the family is adopted, the children often support each other as adoptees, however much they may quarrel about other matters. For example, if one of them starts to talk about how it felt to be left by a birth parent, the other child listens and then also tells how he or she felt. When one child speaks of looking different from the parents and how to handle it, another child may tell of his or her similar concern and offer a solution.

Open Records

During the time our study was in progress, the issue of open records was much discussed in the media and among adoptive parents. As noted previously, only a few respondents stated that they opposed adopted persons searching for their original parents after age eighteen. Most spoke in favor of the search, and many said they would be willing to help with it in the future. No interviewee spoke against the search. Those who did speak against it were questionnaire respondents, suggesting that interviewer presence may have inhibited negative responses. All mothers of foreign-born children for whom there were no records concerning their births or families of origin spoke with pronounced relief about this fact. "Thank God there are no records." Or a hugh sigh, and when asked about the sigh, going on to

express feelings of extreme relief. We can infer from these findings
that the subject of finding birth parents is threatening to many adoptive mothers, and that those experiencing the least likelihood of dealing with a search are most free to express their feelings. Current discussions and legal controversies make it increasingly likely that
adoptees over eighteen will search for their birth mothers and that in
some instances birth mothers will search for their adopted children,
either before or after the children reach eighteen.

Children adopted in situations where records exist need to be
helped to gradually understand the laws affecting them. Parents can
answer the question, "Will I ever meet my birth mother?" with responses like, "Maybe you can. Would you like to? Let's talk about
it." In the ensuing conversation, the child can be helped to understand the ways that will be available to search for a birth parent when
the child is old enough. Keeping in touch with the adoption agency
by sending it a yearly picture of the child and a progress report can
maintain the agency staff's awareness of the child. Since the agency
is the adult adoptee's first resource in initiating a search, it will help
the adoptee if the agency has been kept informed of his or her growth
and progress. Because of recent changes and pressures from birth
mothers and adult adoptees, anonymity concerning the birth parents
and the child's whereabouts is no longer certain. This will be an emotionally laden issue for adoptive parents and children as it deals with
the core question, "Are you my real mother?" Open communication
with the growing child is important when dealing with this issue.

The feelings of relief of parents of foreign-born children who
have little likelihood of finding their birth parents must give way to
concern for how these most "rootless" children can be helped to cope
with issues of heredity and ancestry. Keeping in touch with the
agency or individual who arranged the adoption, and with the orphanage or foster parents, may be the best tie to the child's past.
Pictures of his/her early environment and stories about the country
of origin will be especially important. Maintaining the child's mother
tongue may be impossible, especially in the case of very young children, but if it can be done, it will be an asset in maintaining a sense
of linkage with the past, as well as providing the asset of speaking
more than one language. Visits to the country when the child is old

enough may be very desirable, although in some instances it may not be feasible due to distance and expense.

Support Systems

As we have seen from Chapter Five, most mothers in our study reported strong support systems, emphasizing relationships with husbands, extended family, older children within the nuclear family, and friends. Hovever, some of the adoptive mothers in our study lacked wholehearted family support at the time it was most urgently needed—when the child was initially placed. Sometimes this was related to the idea of adoption itself, as an intrusion into the kinship system of the family. Sometimes it was related to the characteristics, primarily racial and ethnic, of the adoptee. Rather than receiving support, these mothers experienced rejection and had to work at building relationships between the child and other family members. Usually, relatives were won over by the child through a gradually developing relationship. Many mothers said things like, "Once they were around our child, they couldn't resist him." The experience of being in the role of grandparent, aunt, or uncle may also have fostered the relationship. To be turned to expectantly and called "Grandma" by a three-year-old undoubtedly exerts a powerful leverage toward a relationship.

Those of our respondents who were aware that they might forfeit family support went ahead with the adoption anyway. We can infer that a strong sense of independence and an unusual ability to cope with adverse reactions from others are necessary for the less traditional types of adoption. Uncertainty of support by extended family is an important issue, as shown by the fact that the responses we received indicated that initial support by family meant a great deal. When it was offered, as it was for the majority of mothers, the respondents reported feeling greatly strengthened. "My mother came with me to Colombia. My baby was sick. My mother helped me to get her to a hospital and we stayed there together until the baby was well enough to come home." In contrast, those who lacked initial support sometimes responded with bitterness. "We've patched things up now. But it is not the same as before. I still feel a scar on our relationship over the way they acted when our baby first came.''

Discussions with others in the family, with the goal of having its members participate more fully in the adoption process, can be helpful. Since we did not explore how adequately our respondents prepared their relatives for the new arrival, we cannot comment on how well such efforts succeeded. Cohesion and support among nuclear family members are essential, but may also present difficulties if the child requires an unusual amount of care and/or extensive aid in adapting to the family's lifestyle. In their efforts to include the new child in the family and help him adapt, it is easy for parents to expect too much from their other children. Pre-placement counseling may usefully include suggestions about preparing others in the family, and post-placement counseling must consider familial support systems.

The support of professionals and adoptive parents' groups is also very important. Fifty-eight mothers reported that they found adoptive parents' groups helpful. One important value of support groups of adoptive parents is that they focus on those who are doing the parenting, enabling them to function more effectively. Therapists whose work was described most positively by mothers in our sample were those who were oriented toward the family as a whole.

Perhaps because the absence of a ''blood tie'' is less threatening to the community than to the family, the number of mothers citing negative responses from the community was very small. Mothers of young children are quickly caught up in relationships with teachers, religious advisers, and other mothers, and the finding that these relationships were largely supportive is significant.

Our data indicate what one would expect in our society: the major physical and emotional demands of child rearing were met by the mother, whether or not she was also employed outside the home. This implies that major support should be directed to the mother as well as to the child. Some of the most positive comments about agencies carried this theme: ''The social worker showed she cared about me, too.'' ''The social worker did not focus just on the child but on the family.''

Relationships with Agencies

Before beginning the interviews, we asked respondents not to name agencies or staff members, believing that this would make them feel more free to respond. Forty-two mothers, it will be recalled, felt they had had good relationships with their agencies, while thirty-three felt that this relationship was negative. Smaller numbers of respondents rated agencies as fair (five) or as neutral or distant (eight). What factors account for such a high proportion of negative responses? The reasons given by the mothers, previously cited, included a too brief period to prepare for the child, feeling deceived about the child's characteristics, concerns over agency intrusiveness, and concerns about the agency's dual function as counselor and authority which could remove the child during the pre-adoption period. Many of the mothers who gave negative responses offered no or few suggestions for improvement. Since these were women who had shown more than an average amount of determination in coping with the obstacles to adoption, how may we account for their lack of suggestions?

Perhaps the competitive nature of adoption is relevant. Some mothers stated that they were prepared to go through anything to adopt a child. "Well, if this is what I have to do, I'll do it," was a common reaction. Adoption opened the door to an experience these women wanted, but the doorway was crowded by others all hoping to adopt. Circumstances made it clear that many would be disappointed unless they persevered with less conventional approaches such as foreign or private adoptions. With their chance of motherhood at stake, it is not surprising that many women put up with what they perceived as negative situations in order to adopt, and it may explain the paucity of suggestions.

Other Implications

When asked, "What else would you like to tell about the adoption?" one theme that emerged was the very high expectations which adoptive parents held for themselves. Perhaps this is a characteristic of the upper middle class to which many adoptive parents in the United

States belong. For those older children whose origins were in poverty, living a middle-class or upper-class life involves considerable change. For parents and children, it involves considerable striving to help the child meet the parents' expectations regarding education, health, and ways of relating to others. Several mothers in our study stated that adoptive parents need to relax more, enjoy their children more, and not strive so hard. They felt that excessive demands upon themselves and their children could impede bonding.

Among the stresses for parents are two implied (and sometimes explicit) questions which agencies pose prior to placement. For the hard-to-place child, this question is, "Can you make it up to him?" and for the prime child for whom parents are competing, the question is, "Can you give him a better home than others who also want him?" The stage is set for striving in either case.

We noted in our sample that the single parents had adopted older children, non-white children, children from other countries, and handicapped children. The literature of adoption agencies is often explicit regarding their policy of placing children with single parents only when no suitable two-parent home can be found. Even though the relationships of the single mothers with their children were reported as positive, most single mothers said they had found it extremely difficult to succeed in adopting a child. We can assume that striving and effort are especially necessary for this group of mothers.

Finding Homes for children

Finally, we may ponder the most fundamental question concerning adoption: how can homes be found for the many waiting children in this country and throughout the world? Adoption is an absurd tangle of a few highly "ideal" families scrambling for a few highly "ideal" children, while thousands of children never come to the attention of adoption agencies. While thousands roam the streets and die of hunger, families seek children and are told there aren't any available for adoption. Foreign adoptions involve prodigious intricacies of paperwork to deal with the requirements of the two countries involved. Partly because of this very detailed and expensive process, only a few children can be dealt with. The personnel involved—

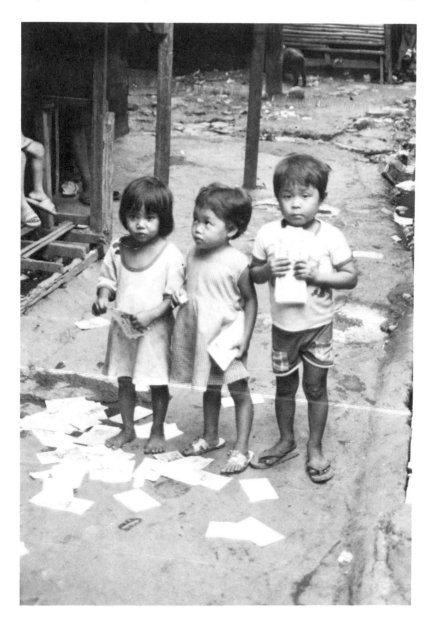

judges, social workers, immigration officials—are all overworked. Yet the children wait, and the families wait. Those who are not young, married, or in optimum health are at risk if they wish to adopt. We can question why it is considered preferable for a child to grow up in the streets or in an institution than to be adopted into a home and family, even though that family is not viewed by agencies as meeting "ideal" standards.

An entirely new approach is needed to help solve the problem. It would be desirable to have an international organization such as UNICEF involved with finding needy children, cutting through some of the paperwork, and helping children who need homes and families who want children to find one another. Although this may sound utopian, no one who has observed the physical and emotional condition of waiting children and attended meetings where scores of adoptive families have been unsuccessful after many years of effort to adopt can fail to note the absurdity of the situation, in which children are the primary losers. What they lose, in terms of cognitive, physical, and emotional development, becomes more difficult to make up with each passing year. Although strides have been made within our country to make standards for adoptive families more flexible, it is still exceptionally difficult for any but "ideal" families to adopt. Since fully one-third of *all* children in the United States will live in single-parent families during some part of their childhood, it seems incongruous that children without *any* families continue to be denied the benefit of a single-parent home while single parents continue to find they are unable to adopt.

Nowhere has the myth of the ideal American family been more destructive than to the lives of the thousands of children previously considered unadoptable. Fortunately, there are those who are seeking alternatives to the present system—agencies who are actively seeking non-white families to adopt the many non-white children, and agencies specializing in finding homes for hard-to-place, handicapped children. As views of who is adoptable become more flexible and more humane, many of these older and handicapped children are now being placed for adoption.

8
When the Adoptee
Reaches Adolescence

Because in our culture adolescence is viewed as an especially stressful phase of development, it is important to consider some issues that affect the adolescent adoptee. In less technologically advanced cultures adolescents become involved in the adult world of work as a matter of course, thus providing them with a place in adult society. In such technologically advanced nations as our own, adolescents require extended schooling to prepare themselves to enter the work force. Those who for any reason cannot sustain this period of schooling are often consigned to low-paying work without opportunities for advancement, or to chronic unemployment. Thus, any possible difficulty that a young person has in following the expected educational trajectory is a threat not only to the youth, but also to his parents who hope and expect him to become self-supporting.

The long period of economic dependence, the exclusion from the adult world, and the coming together of young people in high schools and colleges have given rise to a youth culture, with its distinctive dress styles, particular forms of music, sexual freedom, and often vague and conflicting systems of values.

Although many teenagers have a relatively smooth growing up experience, the public perception of the teenage years is of a period beset with rebellion against authority, narcissism, uncertainty, unwed pregnancy, difficulties with employment, alcoholism, drug abuse, sexually transitted diseases, and suicide. Clearly, adolescence is a time of considerable stress. How do teenages who have been adopted fare in this culture? Let us consider this question in relation to some major concerns of adolescence.

Sexuality

Social norms are highly conflicted in relation to teenage sexual expression, with some segments of society accepting teen sexual intercourse as inevitable, while others insist that it be reserved until marriage. Consensus exists concerning the harm and the hazard of teen pregnancy and of sexually transmitted disease, but recommendations regarding prevention are a source of debate.

Issues of sexuality, and particularly of unplanned teen pregnancy, may have a particular urgency for teenage adoptees, many of whom were abandoned by their birth mothers because of early pregnancy. One teenage adoptee said, "I would *never* want to do to another person what was done to me: I would never want to have a baby I could not keep." Some teenagers with this life experience may be particularly responsible about their sexual behavior. Others may respond in the opposite way, having the fatalistic view that since such events are "in their blood" they are likely to experience early parenthood and that there is nothing they can do about it. The need to have someone of one's own to love may be especially strong in adolescents who have a history of deprivation and abandonment. These young persons may feel a special urge to become parents early in life.

An important aspect of teenage sexuality is choosing and being chosen as boyfriend and girlfriend. Uncertainty concerning genetic heritage and biological family history may lead to confusion about dating. Traditionally, deciding who is the right kind of date hinges upon one's biological parentage, with young people being encouraged to seek others with racial, social, educational, and religious characteristics similiar to their own. The adoptee has two sets of parents: biological and adoptive. Which heritage guides him in dating? The young person whose biological and adoptive parents are very similar in background may have few conflicts in dating, but society typically mandates that any detectable black heritage restricts one to dating within the black community. Hispanic young persons may also face questions. Sometimes, especially if their community is made up of white persons and black persons, they may agonize over whether they are black or white. Those who live amid a large Hispanic popula- tion may find dating easier. "At my high school there are the whites, the blacks, and the Spanish. I am Spanish." Thus did one young per- son resolve her concern about her appropriate peer group.

Attitudes toward sexuality differ among various racial, ethnic, and religious groups. Although this presents dilemmas for all teenagers who meet those of varied backgrounds at high school, it is especially likely to be a concern for teenage adoptees and their adop- tive parents. For the adoptee whose racial/ethnic heritage is markedly different from that of the adoptive parents, the concerns can be com- pelling. These young persons are likely to have a wider than usual range of friends reflecting not only the adoptive parents' social group but also that of the biological parents. Adoptees who live in areas where racial and ethnic diversity exists have opportunities for establishing their identities by making friends among those represen- ting their biological origins as well as among those representing the adoptive parents. Racial, ethnic, and gender identities are sharply em- phasized as young people become involved with the opposite sex. It is not surprising that interest and concern with biological origins becomes prominent among many adopted adolescents.

Searching for a Biological Heritage

In some states adoptees are permitted to begin the search for their biological parents once they have become 18. Jill Krementz, in her book *How It Feels to Be Adopted* (1982), provides many insights into young adults' reasons for initiating the search. Loss of adoptive parents through divorce or death, plans for marriage and parenthood which spark concerns about genetic heritage, and dissatisfaction or estrangement from adoptive parents are all factors which can precipitate the search. Underlying the search is the fundamental ques- tion of identity and a need to establish for oneself the biological roots which are powerful influences throughout life. Krementz describes many reunions of adoptees with biological parents which occur during adolescence, showing that such contacts can help the adoptee solidify a sense of identity. Fortunately, the culture has become more accepting of the need for the search and more aware of the necessity felt by some adoptees to initiate it. Many adoptive parents give the adoption documents to the young person at 18 or 20. The symbolic act of placing knowledge concerning the youth's origins into his hands acknowledges its importance to his understanding of his life. Ideally, the document transfer occurs after many discussions during which what is known about the biological parents and the adoptee's early life is shared gradually.

Krementz has an interesting approach which stresses the value to the adoptee of remembering the past and making contacts, when feasible and desired, with biological parents. Since it is so often assumed that the adoption of an older child (over the age of 5) is far less advantageous to the child than an earlier adoption, it is worth considering the possible advantages of being adopted later. Those adopted later have memories of a past prior to adoption and may even have clear memories of their biological parents, which may result in their having a more realistic sense of their identity. While the memories may be mixed with sorrow and anger, the opportunity during childhood and adolescence to deal with these feelings and with the sense of loss and grief so typical at the time of adoption can help the young person ground himself in the reality of the transitions experienced, in the fact of identity as an adoptee. Such memories can facilitate identity formation in young adulthood.

The value for foreign-born adoptees of seeing their homeland again and, if possible, meeting people they used to know, is currently being stressed by professionals working in the field of adoption. With this emphasis there is a renewed recognition of the needs of the child who has a unique history, and who remembers being in another enviornment.

Independence

This is a pressing goal of adolescence, but amid striving for independence there are longings and also very realistic needs to be taken care of. The adolescent usually does not earn enough to live on his own, and requires guidance and support with the many crucial decisions concerning education, career, and marriage which face young people. Those who were adopted after toddlerhood may delay in seeking independence in order to compensate for the "shortening" of childhood due to their disadvantaged early years. Conversely, youngsters who had difficulty bonding with their adoptive parents may precociously seek independence as a welcome relief from expectations of emotional closeness which they have not been able to fulfill. Independence strivings become further complicated when parental responses are considered.

Adoptive parents have had many hurdles to overcome in adopting a child. Many have gone to great expense (as tends to be the case with foreign adoptions), endured long waiting periods, and submitted to many physical and psychological examinations. They overcame such obstacles because they placed a very high value on parenthood. Many of the children adopted past infancy have required special care, particularly in the first few years post-adoption. Under such circumstances it is usual for parents to over-invest, financially and emotionally, in the child. How will these parents fare when the child becomes an adolescent? Some may breathe sighs of relief, but perhaps others will find the young person's bids for independence hard to cope with because they have had to overcome so much in order to establish the parent-child relationship. The often unexpressed but very common fear of adoptive parents that their children will abandon them in order to return to their "roots," particularly if these roots involve foreign countries and different racial characteristics, may surface at this time and cause parents to over-react to the normal needs of the young person for independence. Such concerns may be heightened if the adoptee initiates a search for biological parents.

Peer Relationships

These are extremely important to adolescents, who need to establish their own networks of friends outside the family. These issues were referred to above in relation to dating, but other factors are also relevant. Most adopted adolescents establish friendships with young people who are not adopted, and whose early life experiences are therefore different from their own. Although adolescents typically become more tolerant of differences as they grow older, some lingering reticence may attach to becoming friends with someone who has been adopted. The adoptee may seek friendship in exaggerated ways, such as by wanting to throw the biggest party, or by impressing age-mates with material possessions. The opportunity for friendships with others who have been adopted is important at this age. The need to be like others is especially strong during adolescence, and finding peers who have had similar life experiences is important.

Anyone who listens to adolescents' descriptions of "home girls" and "preppies" will understand the zeal with which teenagers pursue the outer signs of social class. What kind of walk does the young person adopt? Does he carry a blaring "box" wherever he goes? Wear button-down shirts and loafers? Faced with these badges of belonging to a particular group, how does the adoptee choose? What if the others whom the adoptee resembles physically are poor, and he is not? What are the preferred speech patterns of the group to which he belongs, or would like to belong?

Having real friends requires a solid sense of self, which adolescents are in the process of developing. Lacking such a firm sense of oneself, the individual seeks to merge with a group or with another person (Erikson, 1959).

Extended Family Relationships

Relationships with the extended adoptive family may undergo some changes during the adoptee's adolescence. When he was small, his physical differences from others in the family perhaps seemed inconsequential. He was cute and little, and it didn't matter. When he becomes 16, however, with physical characteristics markedly different from those of the others in the family, their reactions may be different and possibly also more distant. Simon and Altstein (1981) point out that relationships within the extended family are sometimes problematic, particularly during adolescence, when children are adopted across racial boundaries. If a family has denied differences and developed a fantasy that this is a biological child, the fantasy ordinarily cannot endure during adolescence, and its reliquishment leads to stress (Kirk, 1981).

School

When the young person enters high school, changes in the amount of responsibility he is expected to take in relation to school work and teachers occur very suddenly. When a disadvantaged child entering a school system creates added stress for others in that system, the adoptive parents are often highly cooperative and invest a great deal in assisting the child to cope with the expectations of the school. Once the young person is in high school, parental input and control are usually abruptly lessened. The adolescent is expected to carry the responsibility for contending with teachers, doing homework, and so on. For the young person whose parents have been very "active" in negotiating with schools, this change may be difficult for both the adoptee and the parents to deal with.

For a youngster who has had school problems it is essential for parents to keep in touch with high school teachers at first, gradually lessening this contact as it becomes evident that the young person is handling the problem himself.

It is during the high school years that grades become especially important for those who aspire to college. For the child who is older at the time of adoption, school may present a continuing hurdle as more advanced reading and math skills and more complex conceptual thinking are required. A gradual effort to catch up may come to fruition during the high school years, increasing the adolescent's self-esteem and confidence in the future. For the youngster who is not so fortunate there may be tutors, special summer programs in academics, and private schools with small classes. Some adoptees excel in academic work and have a clear entree to the most advanced academic groups in the high school. Since typically children are adopted from relative poverty to middle-and upper-middle-class homes, the importance of education and how much of the family's and the child's efforts and resources should be devoted to it become especially important.

During the early years the parents make these decisions, but in high school the young person must decide for himself how important post-high school education is. If he decides to attend a trade or vocational high school, the adoptive parents may view this as a betrayal of their efforts and commitment to him if they had hoped for college. Realizing that their biological children can also differ from them and adopt differing life paths can make the adolescent's decision easier for them to accept. Decisions about what school to attend will affect the young person's friendship circle, in that peers in a vocational school are likely to be different in values and socialization from the adoptive parents. Thus, choice of high school represents a very crucial decision. The high school is an arena which fosters the young person's individuality and independence, and where he is powerfully influenced by the peer group.

Identity

Developing a firm core of *personal values* is an aspect of forming a firm identity. Values are to some extent influenced by the culture, and adolescents who have moved from one culture to another will have choices to make which might not be necessary for nonadopted youths. Which set of values do I embrace as my own — those of my adoptive parents and my immediate neighborhood, or those of "my people" who may live at a distance, or who may be nearby but are not part of my parents' usual social contacts? As already noted, adoption usually means moving from poverty to relative affluence. When a child is little and very hungry, it seems absurd to ask if he wishes to give up his poverty. He is hungry. He is fed. Questions about differences in culture and values do surface during adolescence. The young person may again seek out a culture of poverty (usually returning to the creature comforts of the adoptive home as needed). Being poor may seem exotic and romantic. It is likely that the young person who represents two different cultures and value systems will have more diverse social contacts than other adolescents as his mobility increases with gaining a driver's licence, and much effort will be required for him to develop his own personal set of values forged from the combination of influences from his biological origins and his adoptive parents' influence and upbringing.

David Kirk (1981) has stressed the importance of acknowledging the differences between adoptive parenting and biological parenting. He wonders about what happens to the child later, once he is grown and is concerned with establishing a family and with other adult problems such as care of aged parents, inheritance, and relationships with the extended family. Kirk believes that in all these matters the young person who has had his status as an adoptee lovingly acknowledged rather than denied will stand on firmer ground in relation to his own identity. He indicates that differences between being an adopted and a biological child tend to be glossed over during the adoption of young children. Kirk feels that the adoptee will be helped in forming his own identity by having adoptive parents who are certain of theirs and who acknowledge their biologic differences from the child. While adoptive parents can help and support a young person in his search for identity, Kirk states, it is important for parents to understand that it is *his* search and *his* identity that is at issue. These theories are in contrast to those which stress the blending of the family in ways which try to obscure actual biologic differences.

Responses to Stress

Many adopted children have faced more than their share of stress early
in childhood. Sometimes the effects of stress are still evident in the
teenage years, requiring continued effort to overcome problems which
began much earlier. Recent research on resistance to stress and
vulnerability to stress is therefore of particular interest to adoptive
parents.

Parents who belong to groups of adoptive parents and their
children have noted that some children who have had traumatic early
childhoods manage to adapt and cope, while others, with seemingly
similar privations, exhibit many problems in adjustment. Recent
studies have indicated that heredity plays a larger part in determining
vulnerability to psychiatric illness than was previously believed
(Bouchard, 1987). Studies of twins adopted shortly after birth into different homes have been an important part of this research. Consistent
findings are that children of a mentally ill parent or parents are at
greater risk of developing psychiatric disturbance than those whose
parents do not have this history, even though the children are brought
up from infancy by adoptive parents who have no history of psychiatric
problems. The previous heavy emphasis upon the overwhelming importance of environment has sometimes led adoptive parents to believe
that if their efforts and resources are sufficient, the young person will
prosper regardless of early life circumstances. The recent research on
childhood resilience and risk factors brings a more realistic view, and
can help adoptive parents gain perspective, a realistic sense of expectations, and above all, lessening of guilt.

Michael Rutter has done extensive research on this topic (Rutter,
1979, 1983, 1987). One of his findings is that two factors are closely
correlated with later behavioral disorders, and that when both factors
coexist, the risk for the child is greatly increased. The first of these factors is family discord (which may lead to a break-up of the family and
institutionalization of the child in an orphanage or foster home). The
second factor is institutionalization itself.

Among these factors which Rutter found to be protective of
young persons are:

1. An adolescent's ability to plan for the future in such areas
as education and marriage.

2. Successful school experiences, which need not be
academic but could be sports or other school-related activities

which help the young person achieve a sense of self-esteem and self-efficacy.

Rutter emphasizes the importance of turning points in the lives of adolescents. Thus, a decision to remain in school can open opportunities for employment and a more satisfactory life. Selecting a nondeviant mate can be a powerful factor in developing a satisfactory life. Teen pregnancy, with its severe effects upon the education and aspirations of young women, is an example of a turning point which is negative in its consequences.

Rutter (1987) has done further research on risk factors for psychiatric disorders in young persons. He identified the following factors:

1. Severe marital distress between the young person's parents

2. Low social status of the young person's family

3. Overcrowding in the home due to large family size

4. Paternal criminality

5. Maternal psychiatric disorders

6. Placement of the young person in an institution or foster home

By being in a stable home such negative results as teen pregnancy and dropping out of school may be avoided, thus opening up opportunities and possibly changing the life trajectory of young people. Research corroborates the importance of avoiding, if possible, any further exposure to factors which already place children at risk, such as marital strife and placement (temporary or otherwise) in institutions and foster homes.

The Adopted Adolescent—Positive Aspects

Much of the discussion among adoptive parents about adolescents centers on the problems they present. Certainly, the adopted adolescent may present complexities to challenge the parents. However, there are pluses to having an adopted adolescent in the family. Perhaps most important is the opportunity for growth not only for the young person but also for the family. The adopted adolescent *is* different from the adoptive family. He has a different genetic make-up, and may be of another racial or ethnic group. The presence of such a distinctive young person within the family challenges the family to become thoughtful and concerned about what it means to be a family. After several children have grown up together, seen each other gradually cope with the community, the school, and the peer group, a loyalty often develops among them which has nothing to do with having the same nose shape or the same eye color or looking like Aunt Martha. It is more akin to the deep bonds which form among groups who have to fight their battles together, making it is what counts.

It may even be easier to foster individuality in a young person who clearly looks different from the parents, thus reminding them of his uniqueness. While photos of adoring parents gazing upon their beautiful children are common and very touching, adoptive parents also gaze upon, adore, and feel a physical, caring bond with these children who are physically very different from themselves. The process of letting go of the old parent-child relationship and forming a relationship of equals may be facilitated by the child's differences from the adoptive family. His physical appearance emphasizes that he is his own person.

Adolescence very often is the time when the whole effort seems really worthwhile. It can be the time when grades suddenly improve and the youngster begins to be motivated toward school accomplishment. It can be the time when social life becomes richer and more varied, when dating begins, when prom dresses and tuxedos make their appearnce. Parties have a special significance during adolescence, and planning for and holding a party can be very satisfying. Adolescence can be a time when the young person begins to relate to the environment in ways which share and show appreciation for parental efforts and interests. A daughter who ignored the flowers for years suddenly admires a rose and picks some for her room. She begins to help with gardening. A mother who has fed birds for years without her children noticing is delighted when a 15 year old sees a bright red cardinal and calls it to her attention. Seeing a play together can be shared fun without all the fuss about monitoring behavior which used to be needed.

If it is natural for parents to worry how their biological child will turn out, it may be especially worrisome to adopt someone and wonder how the child will be when grown. Adolescence shows how he will be. Personality matures, physical appearance as an adult becomes definite, and there can be vast relief. Yes, she's doing fine in school. Yes, he's dating nice girls. And yes, it looks as though this young person is well on the way to being self-supporting. There may also be indications of affection and appreciation for the family which the youngster develops with maturity. The young person begins to give in a more mature way, showing an awareness of the needs of others.

For many adoptive parents there is an initial sense of risk in accepting a child who may arrive with many developmental delays and emotional problems resulting from neglect and even abuse. For these parents adolescence may be the period when they begin to see that what they have done has worked. Their teenager is functioning, is coping, and the family is clearly a going concern. The satisfactions are enhanced when the young person had many problems to overcome, and when reflection on the probable trajectory of this child without adoption is considered. For instance, a child from a foreign orphanage where there was little food and very little care, and where children leave at the age of 13 to go to work, becomes truly unrecognizable in this healthy, happy-go-lucky, very well-fed teenager. Recognizing the differences in intellectual development that result from education, and considering what this child would have been like with only the standard three years of rudimentary learning typical among the poor in underdeveloped nations, can bring joy and feelings of gratitude that the child has been able to manage the transition and now has a richer life before him. When the young person is caring and nurturant toward a younger child or toward a pet, the feeling of gratitutde may increase with the realization that the child is reflecting the nurturance received, and is now able to nurture others, with all that this implies about developing a future parenting role.

The varied contacts which the adolescent brings into the family serve to enrich the family and to broaden its social perspectives. The young adoptee who is from another racial or ethnic group also has his horizons broadened beyond those of biological origins.

Troubled Adolescent Adoptees

For some parents and adoptees the situation at adolescence is not so positive. Instead of a blossoming there is chaos, and instead of fruition there is frustration. Since adolescence is stressful for both teenager and parents, sometimes the additional strains related to adoption are too severe to allow for a smooth transition. Fortunately, more realistic attention is being paid to this possibility, as evidenced by such authorities as Claudia Jewett, who speaks frequently on "What to do when the dream disappears." This section will be devoted to those whose adolescents are troubled, and for whom the period is one of frequent stress.

Claudia Jewett is one of the most vocal and realistic of authors addressing the "limits of the dream" (Jewett, 1978). She points out that the dream of seeing the child progress and develop as the parents had hoped does not always materialize. Recognizing the limits of the dream typically occurs during adolescence, when the child's assets and deficits become clearer. By this time parents have had opportunities to obtain various special medical therapies.*

With the realization that all of an adolescent's problems are not likely to be solved, at least not while the young person is living in the parental home, the parents must either relinquish or modify the dream, and in the process will go through loss and grief. This is an exceedingly painful experience, but it can have very positive outcomes. The parents begin to apportion resources of time and money more carefully and with a realistic view of what is likely to help. Ceasing to push and expect from the child more than he can reasonably accomplish can help parents find ways to enjoy the young person as he is. With less pressure in the relationship, some problems previously thought insurmountable may improve. Sometimes, however, parents wait too long, and deny too long, with the result that the combination of adoption issues and adolescent issues seems overwhelming, and comes at a time when the parents are already feeling financially and emotionally spent. Unfortunately, the rose-colored glasses approach which may have been used in the preadoptive counseling encourages unrealistic thinking in view of the young person's actual situation. Somehow a more realistic balance must be achieved which allows for the possibility of growth and improvement while recognizing the real financial and emotional limitations of the family, and the legitimate needs of the parents and the other siblings, which were held off to help the adoptee, also require attention.

It is not just the issue of adoption which can tarnish the dream. It is the circumstances which precede adoption when the child is adopted past infancy. Michael Rutter (1985) has studied disadvantaged, institutionalized adolescents extensively. He studied a sample of 94 institution-reared white girls, aged 7-12 years, two-thirds of whom had been admitted to an institution before the age of 5. The institution was very adequate in nutrition, education, and recreation, but it had a very high turnover in care givers. This turnover was hypothesized to

---

*Helen Featherstone has published an exceptionally useful book, *A Difference in the Family* (1980) on caring for children with special problems.

have negative effects upon the girls' development. Eighty-one of the 94 girls were followed in a longitudinal study. A matched non-institutional sample was used for comparison. The girls in both samples were studied first at ages 7-12 and later in their twenties. Over one-half of the institutionalized girls were rated disturbed, compared with 6 percent of the controls. Twice as many of the institution-reared girls as those in the control group became pregnant before the follow-up interview. There were no pregnancies in the control group before age 19. Forty per cent of the institution-reared girls were rated poor mothers when they became parents; few of the controls were rated as poor mothers. Other findings were:

	Institutionalized	Controls
Criminality	22%	2%
Broken cohabitation	38%	1%
Personality disorder	25%	0%

The institutionalized girls with the worst outcomes were those admitted before age two who spent their entire childhood in the institution. This study has implications for parents planning to adopt children from overseas orphanages where the quality of life regarding nutrition, education, and recreation may be far poorer than in Great Britain where this study was carried out. It suggests that youngsters who have spent substantial portions of their childhood, and especially their early childhood, in such circumstances are at high risk. On a more hopeful note, it also suggests that those who are in such facilities only briefly and who have extended periods of childhood outside the institution have a brighter prospect.

The ability to control aggression and to channel it may be compromised in some adolescents. Main and George (1984) studied toddlers from 1-3 years of age who had been abused, and compare them with a matched sample without a history of abuse. They observed how these toddlers responded when another child was upset or crying. Eight of the nine abused children responded with fear, threats, or physical assault. Only one of the non-abused children responded in this way.

In contrast with toddlers, adolescents experience a surge of physical strength which, in aggressive youths, can pose a serious threat. Such adolescents need a great deal of structure, an environment where more than one adult is present, and where it is made clear that aggression *can* be controlled and will not be tolerated. Other types of troubled teenage behavior can also occur. Rutter's study (1985), among others, suggests that adolescents who have experienced inconsistent care-taking as children are more likely to experience such difficulties.

What kind of parents are most likely to manage well with a troubled teen? Possibly those who are least rigidly conventional have an advantage over those who place a great deal of emphasis on proper behavior, dress, and manners. Of course, self-control is important, but if one is genuinely upset by a teenager's rudeness or failure to dress or speak decorously, there is likely to be a great deal of conflict and stress which drains energy away from the even larger issues of troubled behavior. The parent who becomes able to work with psychologists, social workers, and the police can be helped by these contacts, while parents who carefully shield themselves from such contacts out of feelings of humiliation and shame cut themselves off from needed help. The parent who can go into ordinarily unacceptable neighborhoods to look for the young person and bring him home, and who can meet those young persons with whom the teen "hangs out" will be more aware of the environment the teen is involved in, and more realistically aware of the problems the teen is facing.

Troubled teens tend to seek out others who are also in difficulties. If an adopted teenager has been abused or abandoned in early life his self-esteem is likely to be very low, which can lead to choosing deviant peers. If poverty has been in his early background, the teenager sometimes will seek companionship in the poorer sections of cities, perhaps feeling more at home and accepted in that environment. For the parent who has "done everything" to make up for and reverse many problems it may come as a shock that the adolescent goes out of his way to seek out poverty or social deviance. This can lead to despair and a feeling of losing the relationship with the young person, despite all the effort and sacrifice which have been made. Understanding that this behavior may represent the young person's search for himself, for his appropriate peers, and for his own roots helps in managing the daily worries over where he is, what he is doing, and with whom. Out of this very troubled time can emerge a more settled, more related, and more socially aware young adult.

Many freedoms are granted by society on the basis of chronological age. Once the adoptee is 17 (or whatever age is required in his state), he is eligible for a driver's license, whether or not he is emotionally more like a 12 than a 17 year old. Parents have fewer and fewer opportunities to intervene and explain as the child matures. The carefully constructed controls and special arrangements made by parents to help the child cope are no longer suitable. A very immature teenager may need a "sitter" as much as when he was eight. Possibly an older responsible young person can come in as a companion, rather than as a sitter, to help provide companionship and stability.

Some suggestions for Parents of Troubled Adolescents

1. Find support, even in places where you are not used to looking. For instance, a single parent in the inner city is often especially sensitive to the issues of single parenting. If your youngster has wandered into a poverty environment, you may have an opportunity to meet the parents of some of his associates, and you may find more support and genuine understanding than you are likely to experience in an upper-middle-class neighborhood.

2. Find agencies and make contacts. Drop the false pride. Acknowledge the feeling, "I can't believe I'm here."

3. Remember that because the youngster is adopted and had a hard early childhood does not excuse his poor or deviant behavior. This will be forcefully demonstrated by others as the child grows up when others in the community have forgotten about his past and his adoption and see only his behavior. You will be blamed as an ineffective parent. These people are responding to how he is now; they do not know the progress made over the past years, which paints a more positive picture of your parenting.

4. Acknowledge the importance of positive peer pressure; use strategies to put your youngster in touch with positive teens in a structured situation. A summer day camp is an example. Left to hang about the streets in summer, the troubled teen is easy prey to deviant youths whose acceptance he may seek.

5. Consider the school and its teachers. This child will probably do best with teachers who are active, forceful, interested, and intervening, rather than with timid, retiring teachers who are likely to

be viewed as easy marks, and thus tempt the young person's aggression and other deviant behavior. Try to find a school which is strict, which emphasizes positive values, and where immediate feedback is given if the youngster is overstepping rules.

6. Look for community groups, such as the Boy or Girl Scouts, the Y, and others, which help young people find companionship with adult supervision, and which foster self-esteem. Help the young person keep busy. Finding definite responsibilities for the young person may be difficult but it is worth the effort.

7. Avoid becoming involved in what the youngster "deserves" for poor behavior. This leads to punitiveness. The emphasis instead must be on measures likely to be effective in leading to changed behavior.

8. Try for punishments which are time-limited so as not to drag on and involve the whole family in tension. For a teen who will not remain at home it is useless to shout, "I'll ground you for a week." Instead, unplugging and putting away his phone or radio is possible and can make the point.

9. Figure out whose punishment it is. Try to punish in ways that do not punish the entire family, yourself included. For example, use other approaches besides staying at home with a furious teen.

10. Reserve battles and confrontations for bottom line necessities. Once into a confrontation you must stand firm, and you cannot do this continually without becoming exhausted.

11. Avoid letting the young person see how unhappy he is leading you to feel, as it will be used as a basis for manipulation. You will need to develop a very thick skin.

12. As time goes on, others in the community will get tired of the kid and his problems and also perhaps tired of you and your efforts toward help and understanding. Sometimes it is helpful to move him to a new camp or a new school and start over.

13. Learn to take breaks, as long as you can provide adequate supervision. A weekend or an evening out is a must to keep some normal perspective. Try not to let your social life revolve totally around the problems of young people.

14. Young people in our culture are very materialistic. Expect to be asked for more, not less, even though the teen is acting up. Set some firm limits about what you can and are willing to give of costly material items. These issues become especially strident during the high

school years, when expectation of a private telephone and TV and car have become commonplace in many communities.

15. Regardless of any physical, racial, or ethnic differences between you and your teenager, he is *your* child. Make this clear on all occasions when the teen accuses you of not understanding his situation. The values you teach are your values. The house rules apply to him as well as to his siblings. If this is not stressed, the youngster may manipulate you into abandoning your standards and your parental role. If this happens, he, as well as you, will lose.

16. Become as unflappable as possible about minor issues which are clearly being used to provoke an argument. Learn to differentiate levels of seriousness of behavior. Using street slang is not of the same magnitude as becoming pregnant during the teen years.

17. Never apologize for your own ethnic or racial background or other aspects of your upbringing. Nothing will be gained by putting yourself down, and the teen who is aggressive or manipulative will perceive this as weakness and exploit it. You have a right to your own background, as he has to his.

An important aspect of parenting a troubled teenaged adoptee involves realizing that non-adopted teens have difficulties too, often for much less discernible reasons than your child. This is a stressful time for both teen and parents whether adoptive or not. It is also important to remember that as later adolescence and young adulthood arrive the young person may begin to show the stability and the motivation which you have been hoping to see. In our society with its extreme materialism and its basic lack of support for families (as evidenced, for instance, by the lack of affordable stable day care) sometimes parents simply relinquish their troublesome teens.

As we read about teenaged runaways it becomes clear that many have been evicted from the parental home by parents who can no longer tolerate the strain and who cannot or will not find help and support to assist them to weather this stress. The adoptee already has a history of not belonging in the family (in contrast with the non-adopted child who may daydream about not belonging). Because of this history of having begun life somewhere else it may be easier for the teen and the parents to view relinquishment as a solution. Recognizing this increased possibility may assist parents to think especially carefully before acting upon wishes to be free of a young person who is a center of family chaos. Teens are changeable, and the next year can bring progress previously viewed as impossible. In private moments of reflection on the circumstances of the teen's early life the parent may wonder not at how badly he/she does, but at how well.

Relationships with Parents and Siblings: Some Additional Considerations

As the adolescent matures he asks not only "Who am I?" but "Who are my parents?" The question of parentage which probably was satisfied at an earlier age with brief explanations now requires more mture consideration, such as"What does it mean to me not to know my biological parents?" "How important is it to me to try to find them?" These are questions which only the adoptee can answer. Feelings about having been adopted are likely to become acute as the young person struggles with these fundamental questions. While some young adoptees dwell upon their good fortune at being adopted, others may feel anger that they have additional tasks to master at what is already a stressful time in their lives. Since biological parents are not ordinarily available as targets for the anger, the adoptive parents may receive not only the anger at themselves, but also that intended for biological parents.

Adoptive parents may, if they adopted an underprivileged child, reflect on what the child was like upon arrival; malnourished, ill, developmentally delayed. Certainly he was very unlike the ebullient, healthy teen he is now. It is natural for parents to look for some gratitude. However, showing gratitude to parents is not a prominent characteristic among adolescents, who tend to be critical and rebellious. The child did not perceive himself, at the time of adoption, the way the parents did. He was just himself. He did not view himself through the eyes of parents concerned for his health, development, and future. He thus lacks the comparisons which they can make. Being reminded of how scrawny or ill he was does nothing for his self-esteem, nor does being reminded of his former poverty inspire him to be less picky about his meals. The search for gratitude will have to be relinquished by the adoptive parents. One day it may be expressed quite spontaneously, and if so, will be treasured. In the meantime the parents must nurture themselves with their own realization of how far the young person has come, and of the part they and others, including the adoptee, have played in bringing this about.

Acceptance of responsibility is a common concern during adolescence. Washing one's own clothes, keeping one's room and the bathroom clean, and pitching in with various family chores are important. In our culture the disinclination of adolescents to involve themselves in these tasks is legendary. Adopted adolescents, if they feel their childhood has already been shortened due to neglect, may be especially resistant to carrying out household tasks. A youngster who scrubbed floors in an orphanage before the age of eight may believe he has earned the right to be waited on, especially since his adoptive parents doubtless served him much more than he was accustomed to, on his arrival. Helping at home may become an incendiary issue if the young person views it as tantamount to a return to his former lowly and insecure status, rather than as a mark of accepting mature responsibility.

Adolescence is, above all, a time of sudden and profound change: in appearance, and sometimes in behavior. Consider the situation of a very deprived young child who arrives to join a middle-class family. The youngster is thin, his hair is thin and lifeless, there are orthodontic problems. In short, the child is far from being the most physically attactive member of the family or school class. It is quite a transformation, not only physically but also in relationships, if the child suddenly blossoms to become the beauty of the family. Siblings who previously were asked to do extra to help the needy new arrival may now find themselves feeling left on the sidelines by a startlingly attractive brother or sister. One quickly begins to hear the words, "Life isn't fair." The parents will experience a challenge in helping the siblings deal with their feelings of envy and competition. Parents themselves may have some twinges of distress if they see a child who caused much family turmoil and required much extra effort "walk away with the beauty prize" while others who demanded less and cooperated more seem more ordinary in appearance. The fact of biological difference can in itself add a touch of the exotic to a youngster clearly different physically from others in the family. Similar issues can arise if the young adoptee develops some unusual academic or artistic talent which surpasses that of his siblings.

On the other hand, the unfolding of the duckling into a swan immensely increases the adoptee's self-confidence and ability to handle himself in varied situations. Because our culture places great emplasis upon physical apperance, such positive changes can seem to present a whole new position in life to the adolescent. In contrast, if the young person develops physically in a way less socially accepted, the added stress of not measuring up to ideals of physical attractiveness will deal another blow to the young person.

Coping with the teenage years or any other stage can be enhanced if the parents realize that enjoying the process is important. Shared fun and good times help parents accept the young person as he is, without a constant emphasis upon trying to change him. Taking up the armor for a battle against illness, nutritional deficiency, educational lags, and so on requires enormous courage and perseverance. Without some humor and time out and mutual afection and acceptance, it can unfortunatley become a grim kind of battle with a gradual loss of the gentleness and ease which are so essential in relationships between young people and their parents.

A major aspect of parenting any adolescent is the realization that, with the coming of the twenties, the young person has left childhood and adolescence and is preoccupied with the affairs of young adults: earning a living, establishing a home, beginning a family. The scene changes irrevocably, and there is no going back to an earlier stage, except in memory. The child is now grown, and the obstacles to his progress that parents saw have either vanished or are now the province of the young person, for his concern. The adoptive parent can take a quiet and very private kind of pride in his son or daughter, knowing as he does the effort and the struggle which were required. Those moments of pride do not need to wait for a birthday or graduation, but can come quite spontaneously, as this child who seemed constricted to a very narrow life now shows a fullness of spirit and a buoyancy, a mirth, and a warmth which never seemed possible.

Adopting a Teenager

Because our culture reinforces the difficulties of adolescence, making this a stressful time not only for parents but also for young people, many are astonished at the idea of adopting a teenager during this tumultuous time. Christopher Lasch (1978) has spoken strongly about our culture, which fosters hedonism and diminishes authority and self-restraint. He describes the difficulties young people face amid the unclear and conflicting values of our highly mobile, very materialistic society. Adopting a teenager seems like the ultimate contradiction of cultural norms, when we realize that the teenage years are in fact the most expensive for parents, emotionally and financially. Regardless of the young person's former background, once adopted in a middle-class home, his demands for the perquisites of the "comfortable" adolescent life come to the fore very quickly: a phone of one's own is a necessity, as is a personal color TV, and once one is 18, a car can hardly be done without! The issue of post-high school education also looms large at this age, and while the teen may not make strident overt demands about education, the parents will be concerned about preparing the young person for future earning; this usually involves some post-secondary education. It is not surprising, then, that a plan to adopt a teenager is met with surprise and shock by friends and relatives. Nevertheless, some people are particularly interested in parenting teens, perhaps because they are more independent, are able to participate more fully in various family activities, and come into the family with an awareness of the process of adoption which is being undertaken and thus may be more ready and able to participate in this process. Claudia Jewett (1984) has stressed the need of teenagers for adoption. Many teenagers reside in foster homes or group homes, following a series of placements which has left them bereft of any consistent parenting. These teenagers usually have an extraordinary need for nurturance, along with their natural teenage rebelliousness. The parent of a newly adopted teenager must be prepared for much fluctuation between dependence and independence, since earlier dependency needs typically have not been adequately met.

Jewett stresses the importance of participation by the teenager in the decision to be adopted. If the young person wishes the placement, and if parents sincerely wish to adopt a teen, the arrangement can be very satisfying. It is essential for parents to realize that they will not be the only parents of this person, but that the parenting role must be shared with the persons who carried this responsibility earlier in the youngster's life. It is natural for him to speak of his earlier parents, and essential for the new adoptive parents to recognize the importance of those relationships. It is important not to compete with them ("Look how much better you have it here") or to try to supplant them ("Forget all that; you're here now"). The relationship must be recognized for what it is, without placing the teenager in a younger, more dependent position than is appropriate, in order to gratify parental needs.

The advantages of such placements are that the young person is well aware of the process, aware that he has choices, and is an active participant who may make an effort toward a successful relationship. Those who adopt teens also recognize that family ties and nurturance typically extend into adulthood, and can be mutually beneficial. Amerasian adolescents who come to this country to complete high school because they are shunned in their native lands, are examples of teenagers for whom permanent homes are sought. These arrangements are termed permanent foster care, and may carry a subsidy.

A further important advantage of adoption during adolescence is that adolescents typically recapitulate many developmental tasks, such as learning cooperation, intimacy, industry, and trust. Adoption offers an opportunity for the young person to heal past hurts and to have a better chance for a mature adulthood.

Conclusion

As adoptees move through their adolescent years, ordinarily the age-related concerns take priority over the issues of adoption. The young person is enveloped in peer relationships and educational and vocational aspirations. Parents are concerned with the expense of all the young person needs and wants. The focus on adoption tends to fade, giving way to the strong demands of the launching period of young adulthood. Whether the young person is adopted or not, adolescence is the last opportunity for parents and their sons and daughters to be together before the inevitable changes occasioned by moving from home, marriage, career, and so on. The opportunities for good times, for a family vacation, for enjoying one another's company become more precious at this time. Ideally, parents experience fulfillment that their job has been done well, and satisfaction in the young person as he is. While dissatisfaction with home and with parents are common among young people at the time of leaving home, it is likely that these attitudes asist them in making the break with home, and in assuming greater independence. In ensuing years they too may look back with pleasure and a sense of accomplishment at their earlier years.

9

Adoption Update

Since we published the results of our study on the bonding process between adoptive mothers and their children in 1983, many societal trends and changes, including in vitro fertilization and surrogate motherhood, have thrown the process of adopting and attaching to a child into a new light. New issues concerning adoption are complicated by the rapidly changing and as yet unstable legal and ethical precedents concerning new modes of becoming a parent. Some of these issues need to be considered as they relate to our study's findings.

In addition, much clinical practice and research concerning the adoption process has occurred or been published in the period since we did our study and published the first edition of our book. Some research findings and some current thoughts of psychologists, social workers, and nurses who work with adoptive parents and children have supported the findings we reported in the book and some have not. Many, however, are relevant in reconsidering the impact of our study and the theoretical suppositions we developed from our data concerning how parents "bond" to their adopted infants and children.

How Well Does Adoption Work?

Our study and the questions we developed for our interviews and questionnaires were based upon a major assumption: that the process of attachment to a biological infant has many similarities to (and some
variations from) the process of attachment to an adopted infant or
child. The bonding theory of Klaus and Kennell (1976) became a
theoretical backdrop for us to look at the manner in which mothers
bonded to an adopted child. However, that same theory of bonding in-
herently precluded "proper" bonding between adoptive mothers and
children, a notion which we rejected. According to the bonding theory
of Klaus and Kennell, the mother has a "sensitive period" after the
birth of her infant. During this time, she is most available to attach to
her infant. If this time period is "missed," as often occurred under
maternity unit management prior to the mid-1970's, the mother is
supposedly at a disadvantage in developing a strong bond to her baby.
This "defective bond" then, might affect the relationship of the
mother and child thereafter. Since an adoptive mother did not
biologically "birth" her infant or child, and thus had no "sensitive
period," how could she or the adoptive father "bond" to the child? We
believed that true attachment occurred in adoptive families, and was
just as strong and viable as attachment in biological families.

Based on our belief, we raised and answered several questions
concerning: the nature of the process of bonding to an adopted infant
or child, the factors that made for an easy or risky attachment process,
the similarities and differences between biological and adoptive attachment, and the conditions under which these variations occurred.

In the past few years, many people have raised questions concerning Klaus and Kennell's original formulations on bonding theory.
Several studies, such as one by Svejda, Campos and Emde (1981), failed to find improved maternal-infant attachment with early and prolonged contact. And fathers, who do not give birth (but can be present
at a birth), also were found to have a complex process of attachment to
their infant (Sherwen 1987). "Bonding" programs in maternity units
have grown out of all rational proportion and are based on the most
superficial trappings of attachment theory with little scientific
documentation of their worth. For example, most hospitals now have
"bonding checklists" that ignore behaviors indicating the complex
process of attachment and focus on simplistic indicators such as the
amount of time a mother spends with her infant. Further, nurses are
not trained to observe attachment behaviors, nor is there any research-

based evidence that these myriad checklists measure anything, much less "bonding" between mother and infant. Family members make appointments to "bond" with the new baby in an assembly-line format. Mothers are asked to sign various documents verifying that the hospital has allowed them to bond with their infant. Nurses write in their notes on patient charts such meaningless generalizations as "Mother is bonding to her baby." Bonding in its superficial sense has truly captured the imagination of professionals and lay persons alike. No wonder critics speak of bonding as a form of "superglue" attaching the mother and her baby forever. Bonding in its popularized form bears no resemblance to the extremely complex process of developing affectional ties between family members and a new child.

Klaus and Kennell themselves warned against a too literal interpretation of "bonding." In the preface to the second edition (1982) of their book (now entitled *Parent-Infant Bonding* rather than *Maternal-Infant Bonding*), they state: "...we were distressed when the word bonding became too popular too rapidly and was confused with a simple speedy, adhesive property rather than the beginning of a complex human psychobiological process. For many months we tried to change the terminology to parent-to-infant attachment" (pxiii). This acknowledgement of the complexity of the attachment or "bonding" process indicates that no one mode of bonding is likely. Attachment or bonding occurs in many ways for many individuals and is affected—either positively or negatively—by many factors. Our initial premise concerning bonding between adoptive mothers and their children seems justified.

Other studies and clinical papers concerning adoption shed light on some of our findings. Information developed since we conducted our study can be grouped into the categories to be discussed here: 1) Comparisons of adoptees and other groups; 2) Successes in adoption; 3) Adoption of the older child (the adolescent adoptee was covered in depth in chapter 8; this section will deal strictly with current studies done on children who were adopted at an older age); 4) Issues in adoption, which include ethics and trends, closed vs. open adoption records, replacement of siblings, and surrogate motherhood.

How "Well" Do Adoptees Compare to Groups Parented Differently?

Many studies have compared adopted children with other groups of children (e.g., biological children raised at home, institutional children, and so on) in attempts to see if adoptees are at any developmental disadvantage. Such studies were prompted by observations of large numbers of older school age or adolescent adoptees who were receiving psychological treatment compared to biological children in treatment. In general, current studies have answered that, under a wide variety of circumstances, adopted children seem to suffer no developmental problems across many personal factors.

For example, Tizard and Rees (1975) compared behavioral problems and affectional relationships of three groups of 4½-year-old children in England. One group of 26 children had been continuously reared in institutions since early infancy; the second group of 39 had been adopted from an institution between the ages of 2 and 4 years; and a third group of 30 were working-class children living at home with biological parents. The results of the group comparisons indicated that: 1) the institutional children had different, but no more frequent, problems than the working-class children; 2) the adopted children had significantly *fewer* problems than the institutional and working class children, and 3) most of the adopted, but few of the institutional children were believed to have formed close attachments to adults. Adopted children, in this study, were at a great advantage over institutional children and, it is implied, over working-class children living with biological families. It is interesting to note that the children were all adopted under four years of age. Our findings concerning children adopted under four years and their ability to form attachments is similar.

In another study, Triseliotis (1983) investigated identity formation in 44 adopted and 40 fostered young adults in their 20's. Compared to children who grew up in long-term foster care, adoptees appeared more confident and secure, with fewer doubts about themselves and their capacity to cope with life. Further, for most adoptees, identification with their adoptive families was complete. While adoptees had no doubts about "belonging" to their adoptive families and about their families "belonging" to them, fostered individuals had a completely different perspective. Individuals who had been fostered were aware that their legal position was unclear, that as children their lives could have been disrupted at any point in the placement, and that their foster parents had many fears and anxieties. Despite strong parent-child bonds in many fostering situations, the ambiguous nature of the arrangement affected the foster child's sense of identity. In contrast, adoptees had a strong sense of identity.

Ternay and associates (1985) studied children's personal and social adjustment and their perceptions of the parent-child relationships in three different types of families. Forty-four families in the study had only biological children; 45 families had only adopted children, and 44 families were labeled "mixed," having both biological and adopted children. The goal of the study was to determine whether children in mixed families encountered unique adjustment problems. A second goal was to examine adopted children's perceptions of their relationship with their parents. The findings indicated that to a very small, non-significant degree, children in all-adopted families had somewhat lower adjustment scores than did children in the other two family groups. However, adopted children in mixed families had adjustment scores similar to biological children in both mixed and all-biological families, on all personality measures. Further, the biological children in mixed families did not differ from children in the all-biological families. It would seem that placement of adopted children in mixed families affects neither the adjustment of the biological child nor the adopted child. Even though children in all-adopted families had slightly lower adjustment scores, differences between the children in the family groupings was minimal. It should be noted that the study did not discuss other factors relevant to the adopted children in all-adopted families. For example, the age at placement and current age of the child are just two factors that may affect an adopted child's perceptions.

In another study on mother-infant attachment, Singer and associates (1985) focused on adoptive and nonadoptive mother-infant pairs. Infants were between 13 and 18 months at the time of the observations. Mother-infant pairs included 27 nonadopted infants and their mothers, 27 intraracial adopted infants and their mothers (that is, mothers and infants were of the same race), and 19 interracial adopted infants and their mothers. Findings demonstrated no statistically significant differences in mother-infant attachments between nonadopted and intraracial adopted pairs, or between intraracial and interracial adopted pairs. Interracial adopted mother-infant pairs seemed to have more insecure attachment than nonadopted pairs. Further, mothers of adopted infants of a different race expressed less comfort in allowing others to care for their infant, and perceived less emotional support from extended family and friends. However, no relationships were found between the quality of the mother-infant attachment in any of the three groups and perceived social support, infant developmental level, infant temperament, the number of foster homes experienced by the infant, or the infant's age at the time of adoption. It would seem that attachment, in general, occurs between mothers and infants regardless of surrounding circumstances. Although interracial attachment has some problems, overall, the quality and nature of attachment that occurs between these mothers and infants is very similar in most respects to attachments between same-race adoptive mothers and infants, and biological mothers and infants. Further, the interracial adoptive mothers' perceptions of their support from family and friends is similar to findings from our study. Singer concludes that the supposed higher incidence of psychological problems found among adoptees in mid-childhood and adolescence cannot be attributed to the attachment relationships that occur during infancy.

Finally, Moore (1986) compared the mean intelligence quotients of two groups of black adopted children between 7 and 10 years of age. The first group (23 children) were interracial adoptees, adopted by middle-class white families; the second group (23 children), who were matched for age with the first group, were intraracial adoptees, adopted by middle-class black families. A comparison of cognitive performance on the Wechsler Intelligence Scale for Children (WISC) indicated that there was no statistically significant difference in intelligence between the two groups. In fact, interracial adoptees, in general, scored higher on the WISC. The authors attribute this finding to cultural and ethnic-influenced rearing patterns in the adoptive homes. However, the study does imply that interracial adoptions have no detrimental effects on the intelligence of the child and may actually benefit it.

Successes in Adoption

In the past, many adoptions were intraracial (same race) infant adoptions. This pattern changed radically in the 1970's at the time of our study. As we collected our data, we found that many adoptive mothers and their children were "non-traditional"—for example, single mothers and couples were adopting children of different races, older children, and handicapped children. Many of these non-traditional adoptions were regarded as situations fraught with potential problems. Accumulated experiences with and research on such non-traditional adoptive situations have yielded some interesting findings concerning how well these adoptions succeed.

Glidden (1985) looked at successful instances of families adopting or electing long-term fostering of retarded children. She interviewed

42 families of 56 cognitively handicapped adopted or foster children to assess postplacement adjustment of the families and to explore the preadoption motivation of parents. Her findings indicate that in successful adoption or fostering situations, the families were familiar with the handicap, were well-educated, and of middle-class socioeconomic status. Motivation to adopt or long-term foster a cognitively handicapped child included biological infertility, religious conviction, and the philosophy that all humans should be nurtured.

Single-parent adoptions have also been found to be successful. Shireman and Johnson (1985) examined single-parent adoptions in relation to potential stresses including financial concerns, sole management of a household, the parent-child relationship, and management of "adoption issues" (such as dealing with biological parents). This study was longitudinal — that is, it followed these single-parent adoptive families over time. Data were obtained from 22 single parents before placement of the child (all children were less than 3 years of age at placement), when the child was 4 years of age, and again when the child was 8 years of age. The data were compared to 29 families with a two-parent adoptive situation. The findings seemed to indicate that issues such as financial stresses, thought to be potentially problematic for single parent adoptive families, may actually be of little concern. In fact, the findings imply that the nature of the relationship between parent and child in single-parent adoptions may make this nontraditional form of adoption ideal for some types of children.

Finally, Dontas and her associates (1985) did a study that indicated that even children who are institutionally reared, under certain special conditions, may still be at no disadvantage with regard to establishing future attachment relationships with adoptive parents. These investigators studied 15 seven- to nine-month-old Greek infants reared in an institution prior to adoption and at the end of a two week placement period. A key factor was that these infants had already formed a bond to a favorite nurse at the institution. When observed after placement, these children had already begun to form an attachment to the adoptive mother during the two-week period. The investigators suggest that because the infants had attached to adults in the institution, none of the previously reported negative effects of institutionalization (that is, depression, detachment, and so on) were found. Further, such institutionally reared infants could form normal attachments to key caregivers such as the adoptive parents, could distinguish family from unfamiliar individuals, and were expected to be able to establish normal relationships throughout life.

Adopting the Older Child

Studies on older children are of two types: those dealing with children who were adopted at an older age, and those dealing with older children (usually adolescents) regardless of age at adoption. It is often believed by psychologists and researchers that when adopted children reach adolescence, certain behavioral problems manifest themselves. In addition, the child who is adopted at an older age, usually over 4 years, may be at risk for development of certain behavioral problems. This is the topic that will be considered here.

Our study supported the notion that children adopted over a certain age may have problems in attaching to adoptive parents. Our interview data seemed to indicate that age four seemed to be an important age — before four, the adoptive mother-child bonding process seemed very similar to the biological bonding process. However, after age four, other factors enter into the developing attachment between mothers and their children. We theorized that, at a certain age, the child needing adoption will have developed his or her own personality and "history." Establishment of a relationship with the mother, who also has a personality and history, then becomes much more complex. Thus, the potential for problems when an older child is incorporated into an adoptive family greatly increases. If the child's history includes abuse, deprivation, and a lack of former attachments with adults, he may be at a great disadvantage in fitting into and becoming a member of the adoptive family. Behavioral problems may develop or become exacerbated.

Other studies support our contention. Sack and Dale (1982) studied case histories of 12 children who had been seen in psychiatric consultation over a 3-year period and who were failing in their adoptive placements. All 12 children had been adopted as older children (average age at adoption was 5 ½ years) and all shared a common history. Some characteristics of these children included: 1) A history of neglect and abuse during at least the first two years of life and usually longer; 2) A behavioral pattern that was intermittently provocative and punishment seeking; and 3) The ability to elicit a sense of bewilderment and betrayal in the adoptive parents. All the adoptive families had been considered competent by agency personnel and all had successfully raised other biological or adopted children. The psychiatric treatment was only successful in salvaging 4 of the 12 failed adoptions. Sack and Dale suggest that more research is needed to better understand the early attachment process in older child adoptions and the impact of the child's history in influencing the child's subsequent attachment capabilities.

Gill (1978) looked at common postplacement concerns of couples who had adopted older children. These parents reported that, after an initial period of attempting to please, the older adopted child often entered into a testing, acting-out phase that presented stressful problems to the family. As attachment gradually evolved, there were periods of regression. Further, the child demonstrated grief, mourning, and anger over the loss of the previous family. The child's emotional neediness and loyalty conflicts produced trying symptoms, and the parent's marital relationship sometimes became heavily conflicted and stressed. Again, this conflict between parents concerning the older adoptee was found in some of our data. Gill suggests that a group support system can help parents deal with these common issues. In addition, she strongly recommends preparing parents for adopting an older child, and intensive postplacement services to ensure lasting placements.

Macaskill (1985) supports this idea in her study, which looked at the difficulties faced by 37 adoptive parents of 5- to 18-year-old children who had formerly been in foster placements. These adoptive families were observed during the first two years of adoptive placement and after the first two years of placement. Macaskill's findings imply that many of the deepest difficulties concerning the placement and integration of the older child into the family unit occur after the first two years of the placement. Macaskill concludes that the study demonstrates the need for long-term post-adoption support.

The studies just cited seem to present a rather bleak picture for the child adopted at an older age. Our data, while indicating that there are risks in the adoption of an older child, also indicated that viable attachment relationships *can* and do occur, albeit with more work and a willingness to overcome problems. A study by Schaffer (1985) supports this finding. This study described findings on children's early development and the implications of that development for future relationships in foster or adoptive families. While investigating many factors related to an older child's eventual success in placement, the investigator's general conclusion was that his findings support the resiliency of children and their ability to overcome early adversities in establishing relationships with adoptive parents.

Issues in Adoption

Many societal changes and advances in the past few years have involved reproductive technologies, procedures, and more. Many of these societal trends have, or have the potential of, profoundly changing the process and nature of adoption. Just as an alteration in the abortion laws produced great changes in the type of adoptable child available in the 1970's, so will such arrangements as surrogate mothering alter the process of adoption. Some issues concerning adoption that are currently appearing in the literature are: ethics and trends in adoption, closed and open adoption records, placement of siblings, and surrogate parenting.

Ethics and Trends in Adoption

For the first time, there is a definite movement of adoption into a prominent position of concern among social and welfare issues. Kirk (1981) notes that as reconstituted families formed by adoption, foster-parenting, divorce, and remarriage become a larger percentage of all families, so does the concept of adoption change from a relatively peripheral item among welfare and social service activities into an item of major interest. Adoption issues are beginning to be regarded as the concern of many millions of persons in North American society. Further, adoption issues are increasingly complex, lacking logical and moral standards for behaviors and decisions. Wiltse (1985) points out some issues which present ethical problems to those who work with adoption. Major dilemmas for professionals include restoring removed children to natural parents, releasing children from the foster care system for permanent placement, terminating parental rights, finding adoptive homes for children with special needs, and giving equal treatment of all potential parents' applications for adoption. These are major dilemmas for professionals.

Closed vs. Open Adoption Records

Another major issue in adoption concerns adoption records. Should they be available to all those concerned? During the time of our study, the trend was toward open adoption records. Mothers in our sample generally voiced qualified approval of this idea. However, many felt that the records should be available to the biological mother and/or adoptive child after the child was 18 years old. Mothers who had adopted children from foreign countries often expressed relief that it was not possible to trace biological parents. Many adult adoptees, during the late 1970's and early 1980's, began the search for their biological "roots" and heritage. Biological mothers joined together in groups and organizations whose goals were to reestablish ties with biological children given up for adoption. Indeed, the societal trend was to favor the claim of biological mothers to know and/or reestablish relations with their biological children who had been adopted—whether as infants or older children. The adoption triangle" of child, biological parent, and adoptive parent was seen as the best way to handle adoption.

Clinicians and investigators have recently begun to question the concept of open records adoptions for infants or newborns. Kraft and others have postulated that severe problems in the development of the newborn may arise (Kraft et al., 1985a), and in the completion of parental tasks when the biological parents have access to the child (Kraft et al., 1985b). According to these authors, when a child is directly adopted as a newborn into a permanent adoptive home, the adoptive parents become the psychological parents for that child. The infant develops a capacity for intimacy, identity, and a cohesive sense of self through a consistent empathetic attachment to the adoptive parents. Thus, the adoptive child's intrapsychic development and the tasks he must accomplish are highly dependent on such a relationship. Kraft et al. (1985a) suggest that open records adoptions run the risk of seriously interfering with the psychological development of the infant. When the infant must relate to a biological parent and an adoptive parent, there may be no consistent psychological parent and hence no sense of self or identity for that child.

The adoptive parents also may have a greater problem in accomplishing the tasks required to move into true parenthood for the adopted infant or newborn where there is an open records adoption. Open records adoption, which may entail having the biological parent in the infant's life, may disrupt the adoptive parent's ability to form and maintain an ongoing healthy attachment to the child (Kraft et al. 1985b). Thus, although open adoptions may be appropriate for the adoption of an older child, when a newborn infant is involved, the ramifications of open adoptions for adoptive parents (and ultimately for the adoptive child) need careful consideration and investigation.

Siblings in Placement

A continuing controversy concerns the placement of siblings: should they be placed in adoptive homes together or be separated? Bellwood

(1985) has proposed a framework to assist the caseworker in making such decisions, based on an assessment of each specific situation. This framework takes into account the degree of sibling attachment, the quality of the relationship between the siblings, the roles the siblings have assumed in relation to each other, the wishes and expectations of the children, and their readiness for family placements together or separately.

Surrogate Parenting

Currently, several state legislatures are considering measures intended to legalize surrogate mothering. Generally, statutes attempt to define and authorize procedures by which an infertile couple and a woman may enter into a contract under which a woman agrees to be artificially inseminated or accept a donated egg, and to give away the resulting neonate to the contracting couple (Sokoloff, 1986). Legislation attempts to deal with the rights and responsibilities of the parties to surrogate contracts. Currently, most laws seem to place the interests of the couple over those of the surrogate (biological) mother, and also above those of the child so conceived. Numerous problems attend the movement toward surrogate mothering. However, as the Kalishes (1987) project in their view of the future, surrogate parenting is here to stay. Since this form of becoming a parent involves adoption and biological birth, it is highly germane to any discussion of trends in adoption.

At present, the practice is so new that there is little conclusive evidence from research or even case histories to document its effects on all the parties concerned. The sensationalized case in New Jersey of Mary Beth Whitehead and the Sterns points up some of the questions to be answered concerning surrogate parenting. For example, what is the status of children in a society that allows such contracts? The laws that have been enacted seem to imply that children are the possessions of their parents rather than persons themselves.

Further, the status of the man who provides sperm for a surrogate mother is unclear. The Michigan Supreme Court has allowed that a man could bring a paternity action to lay claim to the child conceived by his sperm (Winslade, 1981) since he is unquestionably the child's biological father. Another question is whether the contract is valid if the child has birth defects. Who (if anyone) will claim the child then? Related to this concern is the care the surrogate mother will take of the fetus. Will she refrain from drinking and smoking during the course of the pregnancy? What motivation will she have to take care of the fetus, since it isn't hers?

Perhaps the greatest issue concerns the concept of "baby bartering." What constitutes "selling" a baby? Sokoloff (1986) indicates that newspaper advertising for surrogate mothers has increased; fees for surrogate mothers are up to $12,000; and fees charged to infertile couples may be up to $36,000. The infant is conceived, not because the surrogate mother desires him, but because she desires something *from* him, that is, the fee.

Other potential ramifications of this procedure abound: What are the psychological effects on the adoptive parents? On the adoptive child? On other children of the surrogate mother? Or the surrogate mother herself? What will happen to the many unwanted children in need of adoption when it seems possible for adoptive parents to "get" their own newborn? As Townsend (1981-82) notes, "...adoption procedures were established to facilitate giving up an unwanted child rather than to orchestrate its conception." Surrogate parenting will have a great impact on the institution of adoption for many years to come.

Summary

There have been many changes in thought concerning adoption since our study was completed and our book was first published. Much current thought supports our original contentions that: 1) bonding to an adopted child is a complex process that requires the active participation of both parent and child, 2) attaching to an adopted infant or young child (probably less than 4 years of age) is similar in process and outcome to attaching to a biological infant; and 3) attaching to an older child (probably over 4) requires work on the part of parents and children. Yet, problems can be overcome and the placement can be a success.

Many issues in adoption noted at the time of our study, such as open vs. closed adoption records, still continue to be debated. However, new issues, such as surrogate mothering, have come to the fore and promise to have a major impact on the institution of adoption. Individuals who work in the field of adoption need to collaborate with adoptive families to achieve resolution of these issues, and achieve the best possible circumstances for all children in need of adoption.

EXTRACT

Do Adoptees Differ from Nonadoptees?
A Study on Four Measures

Teuta Feinberg*

The purpose of this study was to investigate the differences between adopted and nonadopted adolscents on measures of self-
concept, school functioning, attitudes toward mother, and identity. The study also aimed at determining the effects of disability
and adoptive status on psychological functioning.

The study sample consisted of 52 (33 females and 19 males)
adolescents attending school in the Greater New York
Metropolitan area. The adolescents were heterogeneous in terms
of race, ethnicity, and socioeconomic status. They ranged in age
from 15 to 18 years, with an average age of 16.7, and were in
grades 9 through 12. Twenty-seven were nonadopted, while 25
were adopted. They were drawn from three school populations:
Regular Education (40.4%), Learning Disabled (30.8%), and
Emotionally Disturbed (28.8%), thereby allowing for greater
generalizability of findings than studies using only a clinic or
nonclinic population.

All the adolescents from Regular Education classes were
functioning in the average range of intelligence. Intelligence
scores for those in the Learning Disabled and Emotionally
Disturbed groups ranged from low average to average as
measured by the Wechlser Intelligence Scale - Revised.

The participants were referred by peers, teachers, guidance
counselors, and parents. Participation was voluntary, and
parental consent was obtained. The youngsters were told that
the purpose of the study was to explore the different feelings and
experiences that high school students have about their friends,
family, and themselves.

*Teuta Feinberg, Psy.D., is a psychologist in New York City. This section is a
condensation of part of her doctoral dissertation (see References).

The Measures

Self-concept

The Piers-Harris Children's Self-Concept Scale (PHSCS: Piers, 1984) was completed by all the adolescents. This 80-item scale, which requires yes and no responses, measures self-evaluation, attitudes, and behaviors that impact on the way a person feels about himself (self-concept).

School Functioning

Ratings of school functioning (e.g., adjustment, attitudes toward peers) were obtained from the adolescents' teachers. The teachers were asked to respond to the 300 adjectives on the Adjective Check List (Gough and Heibrun, 1983) as they felt the adjectives described their pupils. One teacher rating was obtained per youngster. The teachers were not told that the purpose of the study was to investigate differences between adopted and nonadopted adolescents.

Attitudes Toward Mother

The Adjective Check List was also used to measure this variable, and was completed by all the adolescents. This scale shows how youths *perceive* their mother as opposed to how they *relate* to her. The adolescents responded to the 300 adjectives by checking those which they felt described their mother

Identity

The Identity Vis-A-Vis Mother Scale (Molnow, 1981) was administered to all the participants in the study. The scale measures the adolescent's perception of how he *relates* to his mother (e.g., "I look forward to being with her").

The Results

No significant main effects for adoption were found on three of the measures: self-concept, identity, and school functioning. In other words, adoption per se did not differentiate the adopted and nonadopted adolescents along these dimensions.

What did seem to differentiate the adolescents, however, was the presence or absence of a disability. That is, classification

(Regular Education, Learning Disabled, Emotionally Disturbed) was found to be a more persuasive factor than one's adoptive status with respect to self-concept, school functioning, and attitudes toward mother. Thus, the adolescents in Regular Education (irrespective of adoptive status) had a significantly more positive self-concept than did the adolescents in the two disabled groups. On school functioning, teachers rated the learning disabled and emotionally disturbed adolescents (irrespective of adoptive status) as significantly more changeable, self-doubting, and hostile toward others than were the youths in the Regular Education group.

Attitudes Toward Mother

The one significant difference between the adopted and nonadopted adolescents was in how they felt about their mothers. The adoptees perceived their mothers as more loyal, helpful, and responsible than did their nonadopted peers.

It was found that the adopted adolescents in the Regular Education group were more positive about their mothers than their non-adopted peers. They perceived their mothers as more reliable, considerate, diligent, responsible, and positive about life.

Similar findings have been reported by Marquis and Detweiler (1985), who studied a normal population of 46 adopted and 121 nonadopted adolescents who were, on average, 16 years old. In that study, the adoptees reported their parenting in terms that were significantly more positive than did their nonadopted peers, and saw their parents as more nurturing, comforting, predictable, and helpful.

Summary

It is not surprising, and in fact would be expected, that of the three classifications, and irrespective of adoptive status, the Regular Education group emerged as the one with a more positive self-concept, a more positive attitude toward mother, and the most age-appropriate behavior in the classroom. In contrast, the learning disabled and emotionally disturbed groups demonstrated more inter- and intrapersonal difficulties.

The most interesting findings to emerge from this study are twofold:

1. The finding that there was no significant difference between a normal population of adopted and nonadopted adolescents with respect to self-concept. The majority of the literature on adoption asserts that adopted persons are "different." Their "difference" has been seen as being the result of an "adoption identity" (Clothier, 1943; Sants, 1974) or a poor self-image (Blos, 1962). Some previous studies have reported that adopted children are more problem-prone than nonadopted children because of their perceived "difference" (Ansfield, 1971; Kornitzer, 1968). Other researchers have found results similar to those reported here. Norvell and Guy (1977) sampled a normal group of adopted and nonadopted adolescents and found no significant differences between the two on self-concept. As further confirmation, Clamar (1978) studied a normal population of adopted and nonadopted girls and found no significant differences between the groups on the measure of self-esteem. The inconsistencies in receipt findings can be attributed in part to inadequate sampling (Lawton and Gross, 1964). The bulk of studies have obtained samples of adopted children from agency or clinical files while nonadopted child samples have been drawn from the large nonclinical population. A preferred approach would be to obtain both adopted and nonadopted persons from the nonclinical population.

2. It would appear that adoptees' positive perception of their adoptive mothers is an important finding given the paucity of research on the effects of adoptive parenting. One can question the accuracy of the adoptees' ratings of their mothers, but research has suggested that reports by children on parents are more accurate than reports by parents on themselves, who, in fact, show a social desirability effect (i.e., an effort to present themselves in ways that they regard as socially desirable) (Devereaux, Bronfenbrenner, and Rogers, 1969).

One could hypothesize that anyone willing to endure the prolonged and involved process of adopting a child must have a strong desire to be a parent and a real commitment to work hard at parenting, and it is possible that this is why the adoptees in this study rated their mothers more favorably than did the nonadoptees.

Directions for Future Research

The study described in this book presents a beginning look at the bonding process between mothers and adopted children. Many other studies are necessary before bonding in adoption is truly understood. However, as important as bonding is, it is but one aspect of parenting. Another important aspect involves the complementary process to bonding—separation-individuation. Future research concerning adoption must not focus solely on bonding, but must also look at the manner in which adopted children separate from parents and become independent individuals.

Mahler et al. (1975) describe a series of gradually occurring developmental phases which encompass the entire process of bonding and separation-individuation in biological children. Mahler describes the biological mother and baby as being in a "common membrane." The phase of separation-individuation begins with what Mahler terms a "psychological hatching" or second birth experience of the infant from the maternal-infant common membrane. The child then gradually begins to separate from the mother (nurturer) and establish a sense of individuality by coming to realize that he and mother are actually different beings. The child next gains awareness of the "other-than-mother" world and the people and things in it. A new level is attained as the child joyfully practices emerging autonomous functions and is able, literally, to move away from mother. Around the second year, a crisis point in separation-individuation is reached where the child now experiences conflict, desiring autonomy but also wishing for the lost unity with mother.

Finally, by about age three, Mahler sees the child resolving the conflict. The child has now established a sense of individuality and a stable internal image of mother which allows him to be separate from mother.

Throughout the entire process, attachment and separation interface—differing amounts of each entity being appropriate during various phases. If the process goes smoothly, the child emerges with the ability to be independent and also to trust and form attachments with others throughout life. If the process goes poorly, problems in attaching and separating may emerge. The adult who is totally dependent on parents or others, and has never symbolically "cut the umbilical cord," is an example of one unhealthy outcome that can result from faulty separation-individuation.

Edward, Cuskin, and Turrine (1901) discuss three problems which may occur during the process of separation-individuation:

1. *Premature differentiation*: When this occurs, the child separates from the mother before actually being able to handle individuality or cope with autonomy. Such a child has often had varied and unpredictable attachments with nurturers and suffers great anxiety about losing others. This fear causes him to develop a veneer of independence to hide true vulnerability.

2. *Blocks to phase-appropriate differentiation*: Impediments to separation may occur in one or more of the developmental phases described by Mahler. For example, when the child should be practicing autonomous functions, especially mobility, the mother may be unable to relinquish her control over its body. By continually picking up the child and restricting its movements, the mother prevents it from practicing skills adequately, and the child does not gain control of and responsibility for its body.

3. *Failure to differentiate*: This occurrence results in psychosis and is so rare that it need not be discussed further here. Suffice it to say that the child, and later the adult, is totally merged with the mother or mother figure and has no individuality at all.

It seems likely that children adopted in early infancy bond and go through separation-individuation in the same manner as biological children. Many older adoptees, however, have had multiple caretakers, multiple placements, and, in the case of foreign-born children particularly, have led lives of deprivation and poverty. It seems likely that these children have had neither a normal bonding experience nor a normal separation-individuation experience. Researchers, then, need to study both the normal process of separation-individuation in the adoptive situation and how separation-individuation occurs in an older adopted child with a previously deviant pattern of bonding and separation-individuation. In this manner, methods can be devised to assist adoptive parents in fostering both attachment and the vital process of separation-individuation.

Adoption and Separation-Individuation

Certain issues present themselves in the adoption of older children which fall within the outlined problem areas concerning separation-individuation and seem in need of further investigation. These are:

Premature differentiation. When a child separates from his mother prematurely, the child covers his anxiety and fearfulness with a veneer of confidence and even aggressiveness. Having had to become self-reliant before he was emotionally ready, and having lacked a close mother-child bond, the child may have difficulty trusting others (a pre-condition to true separation-individuation) and in developing self-trust. Such a child may initially appear very confident and even over-confident, and be greatly admired for his ability to cope with varied environments. As the child becomes more secure and begins to have some basic emotional needs met, parents may find that he becomes very babyish. The child may show many fears—of the dark, of strange places, of entering a room alone—and thus seem totally different from his former self. While it is important for all such children and their parents to have the guidance of professionals to assist them to deal with their concerns of emotional and physical development, it is also important for parents to realize that these seeming losses in coping ability can be a positive sign, indicating that the child is now secure enough and protected enough to go through some of the earlier emotional stages and master them. Conditions which foster the child's ability to master earlier emotional stages and arrive at true attachment and differentiation need to be identified by additional research.

Blocked separation-individuation.   The child who does not have a stable nurturing mother figure during toddlerhood has most likely not been able to explore the environment and become increasingly independent within the security of a firm mother-child bond. Such a child may be expected to exhibit certain problems later in life. For example, he may show age-inappropriate fears of such things as being alone in a room, of the dark, or of getting lost and not finding the way home. A child of ten may well be dealing with the attachment and separation-individuation problems of a toddler. The tasks are more difficult for child and parent because the child is older and larger and is in a situation where more freedom is accorded than would be the case in toddlerhood. Dealing with a temper tantrum in a two-year-old is a far different matter from dealing with it in a ten-year-old who is not easily restrained and whose behavior may make it difficult to ignore his actions. Behaviors consistent with the blocked phases of separation-individuation need to be identified, and parents must be adequately prepared to deal with them. For example, it may be important to provide the degree of safety and supervision which the child needs even though this seems inappropriate for his age. A child of ten who is afraid of the dark needs a night light. A child of twelve may still need after-school care, even though in that family it is expected that twelve-year-olds can cope with their own care for an hour or two until the parents return from work. As the child feels more secure and more bonded to the parents, greater independence will emerge.

The adopted adolescent's intensified concerns with separation-individuation and establishment of independence from the family. The young person who has had firm bonds with parents and who has passed successfully through earlier phases of separation-individuation is prepared by these experiences for the separation-individuation which occurs during adolescence. The child who has experienced difficulties early in life in bonding and separating is likely to need additional support and guidance during adolescence. In addition, adolescents who are of different race and ethnicity from their parents and who look very different from them may find this developmental phase especially difficult. The task of differentiating themselves from parents and seeking their own identity can, on the other hand, be strengthened by parents who clearly recognize and respect the young person's individuality, including his racial and ethnic differences. Peer group relationships may also present added complexities around issues of dating and close friendship to many adolescents who are racially and ethnically different from the parents. Investigators need to understand how the process of separation-individuation varies for: 1) adolescents whose racial or ethnic backgrounds are different from that of their adoptive families; 2) adopted adolescents with the same background as their adoptive families; and 3) adolescents who are not adopted. Methods to cope with role and identity confusion found in many adopted individuals might be uncovered as the result of such studies.

Searching for biological parents. Knowing that one has another set of parents, whether or not one has met them, complicates not only bonding but also separation-individuation. Openness of discussion is essential. The intensity of the children's concerns about these matters may be hidden from the parents unless they make it very clear that it is all right to talk about their biological parents, to discuss the possibilities of meeting them, and so on. Studies of adult adoptees may reveal how having both adopted and biological parents affects the process of becoming an individual.

Some factors in the adoptive situation may foster healthy separation-individuation and these factors need to be investigated as well. For example, the child who survived really devastating experiences prior to adoption may draw strength from this knowledge and experience, and have a basic sense of being able to cope with adversity which may be underdeveloped in some very protected children. The child who comes from another culture, and the child who looks very different from the parents may be helped to see his individuality at an early age. Keeping the child's original culture alive through memories, pictures, and maintenance of the original language are all measures which can foster that child's sense of individuality. The adopted child is not likely to be compared with other family members in terms of heredity, and this further fosters individuality and uniqueness. The child is not likely to hear, as a biological child might, "You take after your Uncle Ned all right. A real ne'er-do-well." "You are just like your grandmother—have to squeeze every dime before you spend it." The adoptive parent may be more realistic and perhaps also avoid some guilt which some biological parents experience. The mother of an adopted child with Down's syndrome will not be burdened with feeling, "It's all my fault because I should never have had a baby so late in life." Parents may be more ready to accept their child's individuality because they know the child was not born to them. The child may be spared pressures to excel in some sport because all the family does, or to carry on a family tradition in music, art, etc.

The fact that adoption is always voluntary and never an accident may also help separation-individuation. The child was sought, and did not just arrive. Thought and planning had to occur before the arrival of the child, all emphasizing that a separate human being was about to enter the family. In contrast, in non-ideal biological parenting situations a child may initially be viewed as an extension of the mother rather than as a separate person, or even as an unwanted burden.

In conclusion, providing food, clothing, and shelter, important as this is, is but one aspect of parenting. Another aspect involves the psychological growth which occurs, optimally, through a relationship with mature, stable parents. Adoptive parents, as well as biological parents, need to assist their child to move through the growth and development stages of bonding and separation-individuation. Assisting in these processes may be somewhat more difficult for parents of older adopted children with histories of faulty attachments and separation-individuation, but it is no less important. Knowledge about these developmental processes in the adopted child can help parents (and professionals) to help children complete developmental phases smoothly. Knowledge can only be obtained by studying these processes. Future researchers need to look to relevant issues concerning all aspects of adoption.

Appendix

Guide for Taped, In-Person Interviews with Mothers

1. How long has it been since you adopted your child?
2. How old was your child when you adopted him/her?
3. Did you have fantasies before the adoption about what the child would be like?
4. Did (or does) your child have any physical or mental handicaps?
5. Is your child racially and ethnically similar to you, or different from you?
6. Describe your feelings when you first saw your child.
7. Tell about times when you began to feel close to your newly adopted child.

8. Tell about times when you felt distant from your newly adopted child.
9. Describe what helped you to develop a relationship with your child.
10. Describe what hindered or made it hard for you to develop a relationship with your child.
11. Did you have an experience of feeling, "Now she/he's really my child"?
12. Did you or are you having a gradual change in your feelings and reactions to your child? Describe.
13. Do you believe the bond between you is: beginning, developing, has developed?
14. What was your experience like with your adoption agency? What suggestions have you concerning the way agencies function?
15. What are your views on adoption?
16. What are your views concerning open records? What kinds of issues do open records raise for you in your relationship with your child?
17. What support systems do you have, and how much actual support do you receive? (For example, from extended family, various parents' groups.
18. What else would you like to say about the process of developing a relationship with your adopted child?

Letter to Those Sent Questionnaires

The enclosed questionnaire has been developed
to gather information about the bonding process of mothers and their adopted children.
Although there is a great deal of literature
about the bonding of biologic children and
their mothers, little has been written about
this process in adopted children and their
mothers.

We are professors of Child-Parent Nursing at
Rutgers University, Newark, New Jersey. We
would like to help professionals working with
adoptive parents and their children provide
better assistance based on adoptive family
needs. We would greatly appreciate your response. Sharing knowledge will help other adoptive parents. Your responses, of course, will
remain confidential.

Please do not hesitate to contact us if you
have any questions or if you wish further explanations about the study.

Sincerely yours,

Dorothy Smith   Laurie Sherwen

Mail Questionnaire for Mothers

(Please feel free to add extra sheets, explaining and adding as you wish.)

1. How long has it been since you adopted your child?
2. Is your child a girl or a boy?
3. How old was your child when you adopted him/her?
4. Has your child any physical or mental handicap? If yes, describe.
5. Is your child of the same race as you? If not, describe difference.
6. Is your child of the same ethnic background as you (for instance, English or Italian)? If not, describe difference.
7. Did you have fantasies about your child before you actually took the child into your home?
8. If yes, please describe them. Also, was the child like or different from the fantasized child?
9. Describe your feelings when you first saw your new child.
10. Describe examples of times when you began to feel close to your newly adopted child.
11. Describe example of times when you felt distant from your newly adopted child.
12. Describe what helps you develop a relationship with your child.
13. Describe what hinders you in developing a relationship with your child.
14. Did you have an experience of feeling, "Now she (he) is really my child"? If so, please describe this experience.

15. Did you have, or are you having, a gradual change in your feelings and reactions to your adopted child? If so, describe.
16. Do you believe the bond between you is 1) beginning, 2) developing, or 3) has developed?
17. Do you think there is anything positive an adopted child has which other children may not have? In other words, are there any pluses to adoption?
18. Do you believe there is anything negative about adopting a child?
19. How do you plan to deal with the negative aspects?
20. Would you describe your experience with your adoption agency as 1) good, 2) fair, or 3) poor?
21. Have you suggestions you would like to make concerning the way agencies function?
22. What are your views concerning open records? Do you believe this is positive or negative? What issues do open records raise for you in your relationship with your child?
23. What support systems do you have, and how much actual support do you receive (that is, from your extended family, parents' groups, etc.)?
24. What else would you like to tell us about the process of developing a relationship with your child?

Children's Questionnaire

(This questionnaire was addressed to the parents,
with an explanatory letter and consent forms. See
Chapter 6 for responses to the questionnaire)

This study will help other children who are adopted, and it will help their mothers and social
workers. I am a teacher at a univiversity. Also,
I am a mother of two adopted children. I would be
very interested in your responses to the questions.
Before you answer any question, it will be
necessary for you to sign a consent form and to
ask one of your parents to sign a consent form,
too.

1. How long ago were you adopted? How old were
    you then?
2. Are you similar to your adoptive mother in
    appearance? Different? If different, in
    what way?
3. If you were old enough at the time of your
    adoption to think about it, did you imagine
    what your new mother would look like?
4. Did she look the way you though she would?
    Different?
5. Were you old enough to remember how you felt
    when you first met your new mother? If so,
    describe how you felt then.
6. Describe times when you began to feel close
    to your new mother (friendly, affectionate,
    loving).

7. Describe times when you felt distant from
    your new mother (angry, annoyed, uninterested).
8. Describe what helps you develop a relation-
    ship with your mother.
9. Describe what gets in the way of developing
    a relationship with your mother.
10. What do you think are good things about being
    adopted (things you like)?
11. What do you think are bad things about being
    adopted (things you don't like)?
12. Were you old enough to remember your social
    worker? How well do you think she or he
    prepared you for your adoption? What suggest-
    ions have you for how children should be pre-
    pared for adoption?
13. What else would you like to tell about your
    adoption?

Please feel free to add extra sheets of paper and
write more if you wish.

References

Abbott, J.H.: *In the Belly of the Beast.* New York: Random House, 1981.

Ainsworth, M.D.: The effects of maternal deprivation: A review of findings and controversy in context of research strategy. In: *Deprivation of Maternal Care: A Reassessment of Its Effects.* New York: Schocken Books, 1966.

Ansfield, J.G.: *The Adopted Child.* Springfield, Il.: Charles C Thomas, 1971.

Anthony, E.J. and Cohler, B. (eds.): *The Invulnerable Child.* New York: Guilford Publications, 1987.

Bellwood, P.: Assessing siblings for family placement. *Adoption and Fostering* 9:33-34, 1985.

Benedek, T.: The psychobiology of pregnancy. In: Anthony, E.J. and Benedek, T. (eds.): *Parenthood.* Boston: Little, Brown, 1970.

Blos, P.: *On Adolescence: A Psychoanalytic Interpretation.* New York: The Free Press of Glencoe, 1962.

Bibring, G.: Some considerations of the psychological processes in pregnancy. *The Psychoanalytic Study of the Child* 14:113-121, 1959.

Bouchard, T.J.: Genes and behavior. *Psychology Today* 21:18, 1987.

Bowlby, J.: *Maternal Care and Mental Health.* New York: Schocken Books, 1966.

Bowlby, J.: *Separation: Anxiety and Anger.* New York: Basic Books, 1973.

Brazelton, J.B.: Comment. In: Klaus, M. and Kennell, J., *Maternal-Infant Bonding.* St. Louis: C.V. Mosby, 1976, p. 42.

Bush, M.: Institutions for dependent and neglected children. *American Journal of Orthopsychiatry* 50:239-241, 1980.

Caplan, G.: *Concepts of Mental Health and Consultation.* Washington, D.C.: U.S. Department of Health, Education and Welfare, 1959.

Clamar, A.J.: *A Comparative Study of Selected Personality Characteristics of Eight- to 12-Year-Old Adopted and Nonadopted Girls.* Unpublished doctoral dissertation, New York University, 1978.

Cline, F.: *What Shall We Do With This Kid?* Evergreen, CO: Evergreen Consultants in Human Behavior, 1979.

Clothier, F.: The psychology of the adopted child. *Mental Hygiene* 27:222-230, 1943.

Cohen, R.L.: Some maladaptive syndromes of pregnancy and the puerperium. *Obstetrics and Gynecology* 27:562-570, 1966.

Detweiler, R. and Marquis, K. Drew University, Madison, N.J. Personal communication, 1981.

Devereaux, E.C., Bronfenbrenner, U., and Rogers, R.R.: Child rearing in England and the United States: A cross-national comparison. *Journal of Marriage and the Family* 31:257-270.

Dontas, C., Maratos, O., Fafoutis, M. and Karangelis, A.: Early social development in institutional reared Greek infants: Attachment and peer interaction. *Monograph of the Society for Research in Child Development* 50(1-2):136-146, 1985.

Edward J., Ruskin, N. and Turrini, A.: *Separation-Individuation.* New York: Gardner Press, 1981, pp. 47-73.

Erikson, E.: *Childhood and Society.* New York: W.W. Norton, 1963.

Erikson, E.: *Identity, Youth and Crisis.* New York: W.W. Norton, 1968.

Fawcett, J.: Body image and the pregnant couple. *The American Journal of Maternal-Child Nursing* 3:227-233, 1978.

Featherstone, H.: *A Difference in the Family.* New York: Basic Books, 1980.

Feigelman, W. and Silverman, A.: *Chosen Children.* New York: Basic Books, 1983.

Feinberg, T.: *An Investigation of the Overrepresentation of Adoptees in the Psychiatric Literature.* Unpublished doctoral dissertation. New York: Yeshiva University.

Fischer, L.L.: Hospitalism in six month old infants. *American Journal of Orthopsychiatry* 22:522, 1952.

Frank, G.: Treatment needs of children in foster care. *American Journal of Orthopsychiatry* 50:256-258, 1980.

Freud, A., Goldstein, J., and Solnit, A.J.: *Beyond the Best Interest of the Child*. New York: Macmillan, 1973.

Garmezy, N.: Stress, competence, and development. *American Journal of Orthopsychiatry* 57:159, 1987.

Gill, M.: Adoption of older children. *Social Casework* 59:272-278, 1978.

Glidden, L.: Adopting mentally handicapped children: Family characteristics. *Adoption and Fostering* 9:53-56, 1985.

Gough, H.G. and Heilburn, A.F., Jr.: *The Adjective Check List*. Palo Alto: Consulting Psychologists Press, 1983.

Jewett, C.L.: *Adopting the Older Child*. Cambridge: The Harvard Common Press, 1978.

Kalisch, B. and Kalisch, P.: Nursing 2010. Paper presented at the Sixth National Meeting, NAACOG, Phoenix, Arizona, 1987.

Kinard, E.M.: Emotional development in physically abused children. *American Journal of Orthopsychiatry* 50:686-690, 1980.

Kirk, H.D.: *Adoptive Kinship*. Toronto: Butterworths, 1981.

Klaus, M. and Kennell, J.: *Maternal-Infant Bonding*. St. Louis: C.V. Mosby, 1976.

Klaus, M. and Kennell, J.: *Parent-Infant Bonding*. St. Louis: C.V. Mosby, 1982.

Kornitzer, M.: *Adoption and Family Life*. London: Putnam, 1968.

Kraft, A. et al. Some theoretical considerations on confidential adoptions: II. The adoptive parent. *Child and Adolescent Social Work Journal* 2:69-82, 1985a.

Kraft, A. et al. Some theoretical considerations on confidential adoptions: III. The adopted child. *Child and Adolescent Social Work Journal* 2:139-153, 1985b.

Krementz, J.: *How It Feels to Be Adopted*. New York: Alfred A. Knopf, 1982.

Lasch, C.: *The Culture of Narcissism*. New York: W.W. Norton, 1978.

Lawton, J. and Gross, S.: A comparison of self-concept in adopted and non-adopted children. *Archives of General Psychiatry* 11:349-358, 1964.

Lipkin, G.: *Parent-Child Nursing*. St. Louis: C.V. Mosby, 1978.

Macaskill, C.: Post-adoption support: Is it essential? *Adoption and Fostering* 9:45-49, 1985.

MacFarlane, A.: *The Psychology of Childbirth*. Cambridge: Harvard University Press.

Mahler, M., Pine, F., and Bergman, A.: *The Psychological Birth of the Human Infant*. New York: Basic Books, 1975, pp. 3-16.

Marquis, K.S. and Detweiler, R.A.: Does adopted mean different? An attributional analysis. *Journal of Personality and Social Psychology* 48:1054-1066, 1985.

McBride, A.B.: *The Growth and Development of Mothers*. New York: Harper and Row, 1973.

McRoy, R.: University of Texas, Austin. Personal communication. 1981.

Mead, M.: A cultural anthropologist's approach to maternal deprivation. In: *Deprivation of Maternal Care: A Reassessment of Its Effects*. New York: Schocken Books, 1966. pp. 237-254.

Molnow, E. *Adolescent Separation-individuation and the Parent/Child Relationship*. Unpublished doctoral dissertation. Univerity of Cincinnati, 1981.

Moore, E.: Family socialization and IQ test performance of traditionally and transracially adopted black children. *Developmental Psychology* 22:317-326, 1986.

Neubauer, P. (ed.): *The Process of Child Development*. New York: Jason Aronson, 1976.

Norvell, M. and Guy, R.F.: A comparison of self-concept in adopted and non-adopted adolescents. *Adolescence* 12:443-448, 1977.

Plumez, J.H.: Adoption: Where have all the babies gone? *The New York Times Magazine,* April 13, 1980, pp. 9-12.

Powell, J.Y.: *Whose Child Am I? Adults' Recollections of Being Adopted*. New York: Tiresias Press, 1985.

Powers, D. (ed.): *Adoption for Troubled Children*. New York: Haworth Press, 1984.

Rubin, R: Attainment of the maternal role. I. *Nursing Research* 16:237, 1967.

Rubin, R.: Fantasy and object constancy in maternal relationships. *Maternal Child Nursing Journal* 1:101, 1972.

Rutter, M.: Psychosocial resilience and protective mechanisms. *American Journal of Orthopsychiatry* 57:316, 1987.

Rutter, M.: Resilience in the face of adversity. *British Journal of Psychiatry* 147:598, 1985.

Rutter, M.: *The Qualities of Mothering*. New York: Jason Aronson, 1974.

Sack, W. and Dale, D. Abuse and deprivation in failing adoptions. *Child Abuse and Neglect* 6:443-451, 1982.

Sachdev, P. (ed.): *Adoption: Current Issues and Trends*. Toronto: Butterworths, 1984.

Sants, H.J.: Genealogical bewilderment in children with substitute parents. *British Journal of Medical Psychology* 37:133-141, 1964.

Schaffer, H.: Making decisions about children. *Adoption and Fostering* 9, 22-28, 1985.

Schechter, M.: About adoptive parents. In: Anthony, E.J. and Benedek, T. (eds.): *Parenthood*. Boston: Little, Brown, 1970.

Sherwen, L.: *Psychosocial Dimensions of the Pregnant Family*. New York: Springer, 1987.

Shiremen, J., Johnson, P.: Single-parent adoptions: A longitudinal study. *Children and Youth Service Review* 7:321-334, 1985.

Simon, R. and Altstein, H.: *Transracial Adoption*. New York: John Wiley, 1977.

Simon, R.J. and Altstein, H.: *Transracial Adoption: A Follow Up*. Lexington, MA: D.C. Heath, 1981.

Singer, L. M. Brodzinsky, D.M., Ramsay, D., Steir, M., and Waters, E.. Mother-infant attachment in adoptive families. *Child Development* 56, 1543-1551, 1985.

Sokoloff, B. Surrogate mothering: In the best interests of the child? *Journal of Perinatology* 6:191-192, 1986.

Svejda, M.J., Campos, J.J. and Emde, R.N.: Mother-infant "bonding": Failure to generalize. *Annual Progress in Child Psychiatry and Child Development*, 49-57, 1981.

Ternay, M., Welborn, B. and Day, H. Perceived child-parent relationships and child adjustment in families with both adopted and natural children. *Journal of Genetic Psychology* 146:261-272, 1985.

Thornburg, H.: Adolescence. In: Neubauer, P. (ed.): *The Process of Child Development*. New York: W.W. Norton, 1978.

Tizard, B.: *Adoption*. New York: The Free Press, 1977.

Tizard, B. and Rees, J. The effect of early institutional rearing on the behaviour problems and affectional relationships of four-year-old children. *Journal of Child Psychology and Psychiatry and Allied Disciplines* 16:61-73, 1975.

Townsend, M. Surrogate mother agreements: Contemporary legal aspects of a biblical notion. *University of Virginia Law Review* 467-483. 1981-1982.

Tremitiere, B.T.: Adoption of children with special needs – the client-centered approach. *Child Welfare* 58:682, 1979.

Triseliotis, J.: Identity and security in adoption and long-term fostering. *Adoption and Fostering* 7:22-31.

Ward, M.: Culture shock in the adoption of older children. *The Social Worker* 48:46-49, 1980.

Ward, M.: Parental bonding in older child adoptions. *Child Welfare* 60:30-36, 1981.

Wilson, M., Daly, M. and Weghorst, L.: Household composition and the risk of child abuse and neglect. *Journal of Biosocial Science* 12:333-337, 1980.

Wiltse, K.: Ethical issues in permanency planning for children. *Children and Youth Services Review* 7:259-266.

Winslade, W.: Surrogate mothers: Private right or public wrong? *Journal of Medical Ethics* 7:153, 1981.

Wolins, M.: Group care: Friend or foe? In: Chess, S. and Thomas, A. (eds.): *Annual Progress in Child Psychiatry and Child Development.* New York: Brunner/Mazel, 1970.

Index

IQ, 170

M

Maternal deprivation (early),
  effects of, 63-67
"Mixed" families with both
  biological and adopted
  children, 169
Monotropy, 63, 94
Mothers
  agency relationships and,
    92-93
  attitudes of adoptees toward,
    103-107, 179-181
  bonding and, 57, 69, 75-89,
    169-171 (*See also* Bon-
    ding)
  closeness factors and, 86-88
  distance factors and, 88-89
  fantasies about child to
    come, 59, 68, 81-82,
    123-124
  feelings about adoption, 94-95
  fetal-maternal interaction, 67
  first encounter with child,
    83-85, 126-129
  older children, adoption of
    (*See* Older child adop-
    tions)
  personality, effects on
    bonding, 68-69
  stresses of, 138
  support systems for, 54, 59,
    60, 82-83, 89-90, 125,
    135-136

O

Older child adoptions, 51, 53,
  69, 115-117, 161-163,
  172-173
  and attachment to parents,
    172
  behavioral problems and,
    152-155
Open records, 90-91, 133-135,
  143-144, 174-175

P

Parent-child attachment, 169,
  170
Parenting, biological vs. adoptive, 91, 95
  overdoing, 96
Parents, adoptive
  social attitudes and, 53-55
  vulnerability of, 47-48
Peer relationships, 145-146
Post-placement services, 125
Psychological problems of
  adoptees, 172-173

Q

Questionnaires for study participants, 189-195

R

Racial differences between
  adopted child and
  parents (*See* Interracial
  adoptions)

Relationships with parents and
siblings, 159-161,
184-185
Retarded adoptees, 171

S

Sensitive period of mother for
bonding, 166
School functioning, 146-147,
179
Self-concept, adoptees', 179,
180
Separation-individuation,
184-187
Sexuality and adolescents,
142-143
Siblings, placing in adoption,
175-176
Single parent adoptions, 50,
138, 171
Social adjustment, 169
Social attitudes toward adoption, 53-55, 69, 83
Stress
in adoption, 69, 137-138
in adolescents, 148-150

Support systems for adoptive
family, 54, 59, 60,
82-83, 89-90, 125,
135-136
Surrogate parenting, 176-177

T

Teenagers, *see* Adolescents and
Adolescence
Teenagers, adopting, 161-163
172-173
Theories about bonding, 57,
69, 166
Transethnic/transracial adoptions, 51, 93-94,
100-103, 120-123,
170
children's feelings about,
101-103
Trends in adoption, 174
Troubled Adolescents, 152-158

U

Unadopted children, 53